PRAISE

THE NEW COP

John has done something remarkable here. He not only reveals the flaws in how institutions discuss "millennials," but also builds a completely new framework for explaining how human consciousness has evolved in a global, digital age. It's an essential read for anyone who wants to survive the next 25 years.

> Mike McHargue
> Author, *Finding God in the Waves*
> Co-host, *The Liturgists Podcast*

Do not miss reading this book. Full of wisdom, research and passion, John Seel helps us to view this tectonic shift toward millennials' influence in culture as a generative opportunity. As an artist, I have seen this shift already taken place in the art world for some time now. The "iceberg" is right in front of us! It's now the churches' responsibility to respond to principles that John carefully traces in this fine work.

> Mako Fujimura
> Artist
> Vision Director, Brehm Center, Fuller Theological Seminary

The New Copernicans is a prophetic warning and wise guide for the evangelical church. Seel's call to listen to the haunted spiritual longings of millennials will help us to join in their intuitive sense of a non-dualistic convergence of God's Spirit moving among us. John is a useful and humble partner in spiritual pilgrimage.

> Richard Rohr
> Author, *The Divine Dance*
> Founder of the Center for Action and Contemplation

No one has done more to reframe my understanding of our current moment than Dr. John Seel. The ideas in this book will change both your understanding of our cultural landscape and your relating to the people who inhabit it— especially those much-maligned and misunderstood millennials.

> Sean Womack
> CEO, Smack.co

We know the Kingdom is always near—it's in the stories that shape us, the journeys that refine us, and the loves that direct us. Yet, millennials have taken to heart this reality in a way the church has not. Can the church learn from her children? In *The New Copernicans*, John Seel has given us an on-ramp. I am beyond grateful for this work.

Chase Daws
Reformed University Fellowship Campus Minister
University of California, Berkeley

We are, I believe, in the midst of a shift in the plate tectonics of American religious culture. A work like Taylor's *A Secular Age* has resonated because it has so accurately uncovered the genealogy that leads to this moment. What has been missing, however, is the kind of careful listening to and nuanced observation of those who are the vanguard generation of this shift. *The New Copernicans* fills this gap, providing important insights into this massive generational shift.

James Davison Hunter
Author, *To Change the World*

I'm a millennial as well as a college professor and a cultural critic, and I find John Seel's way of thinking about my generation compelling and grounded in a generosity that's extremely rare. I wish I could put a copy of this book into the hands of every person tasked with leading the church.

Alissa Wilkinson
English Professor, The King's College
Film Reviewer, Vox

In working with young adults over the past two decades, I have heard many wonder about the future of the church (and our world!) as it relates to the wiring of the "next" generation. *The New Copernicans* is a good reminder that the millennial generation was created for such a time as this! John's encouragement to pay attention and learn from this generation is a helpful construct in understanding how to reach the world for Christ in an ever-changing culture.

Vincent Burens
President and CEO
Coalition for Christian Outreach (CCO)

There are many things going on in this remarkable book, bunches of reasons you should consider buying it. At the very least, it is an insightful cry to church leaders—conservative evangelicals, especially—to more deeply understand the profound cultural changes we are experiencing and how younger adults are often carriers of this post-Enlightenment shift to right-brained, relational ways of experiencing life and faith. It is one of the most provocative books of cultural discernment I've read, and I hope church leaders explore it. But there is more: Seel has walked with the New Copernicans and has listened well. He tells stories ranging from meeting Black Lives Matter activists to the founders of churches that revolve around meals and hospitality, to rising adults who explain why social media is so very important to them. You may not like all that he tells about here, but you will learn much, and you will be inspired to enter more vividly into the world in which we are increasingly finding ourselves, being guided by those who are in the vanguard: the New Copernicans.

Byron Borger
Owner, Hearts & Minds Bookstore

Amidst much clamor and din today, John Seel brings a deft listening skill, winsome voice and humble exhortation to the subject of New Copernicans. A must-read for all those who endeavor to understand both the challenges and opportunities for a generation that is poised to change the world.

John Priddy
CEO and Cofounder, Windrider Institute

Will Christ win or lose the millennials? No question is more worthy of pastoral consideration because the stakes for the future of the church and of basic Christianity could not be higher. John Seel offers highly informed, deep, and appreciative insights into the spiritual lives of the millennials. He shows us older Generation Xers or Baby Boomers how to value the wonderful spirit and faith of a generation that is too often underrated, and that holds the key to the new future of Christian faith and community. Seel has written a magnificent book that every pastor and lay-Christian should read for new perspectives, for practical approaches to outreach, and for renewed commitment to spreading the gospel.

Stephen G. Post, PhD
Professor of Family, Population and Preventive Medicine, Stony Brook University
President, The Institute for Research on Unlimited Love

Copernicus saw something that many people of faith weren't ready for. John Seel challenges us to see millennials as New Copernicans with four on-ramps to spiritual pilgrimage: justice, beauty, sexuality, and spirit. In this much-needed road map for ministry, John helps us reframe these on-ramps for more effectively meeting the challenges of the new evangelization.

Christopher West

Senior Lecturer, Theology of the Body Institute

I spend a lot of time with organizations and leaders who throw their hands up in the air or offer only surface-level prescriptions to dealing with the next generation. John Seel's *The New Copernicans* offers a simple, radical alternative of thoughtfully, humbly seeking to understand how millennials view the world, and to consider the ways in which this might be a gift to us and to our faith. I learned a great deal about millennials, and therefore the future, in this paradigm-shifting book, and I am grateful to John for showing us a way forward.

Michael Wear

Author, *Reclaiming Hope: Lessons Learned in the Obama White House About the Future of Faith in America*

I enjoyed *The New Copernicans* more than I can express. I am a more informed Christian and parent after reading this book. As a producer, I live and work in Hollywood, which is made up of imagination and young artists. Artists are prophets, prophets are Copernicans, and our culture is shaped by our millennial Copernicans. If we don't take the time to understand them, we will be unaware of the trajectory of our nation. That is why I call Hollywood the world's most influential mission field, and John Seel calls this New Copernican reality the church's most pressing mission field. And the missionary's first job is to learn who the people are whom they are serving.

Karen Covell

President, Hollywood Prayer Network

The millennial generation has completely changed everything we know about our culture. The problem is, up to now, the vast amount of research, information, and recommendations are about what that generation gets wrong. Now, John Seel has balanced the scale. In *The New Copernicans: Understanding the Millennial Contribution to the Church*, we now have the story of who they are, how they think, and how it will impact the future of Christianity. It's an incredible book, and one that every leader needs to read.

Phil Cooke, PhD

Filmmaker, Media Consultant, and author, *Unique: Telling Your Story in the Age of Brands and Social Media*

John Seel begins *The New Copernicans* innocently enough, with two unassailable sociological facts about the millennial generation. They are leaving the evangelical church, and they embody a significant shift about how reality and truth are apprehended and lived. Old news, you say. But Seel wants us to reconsider what's really occurring. Young adults are abandoning the church, he says, because the church is needlessly alienating them. And although the church is aware of the cultural shift in thinking and living, just about everything the church believes about it is wrong. "This new way of processing reality," he argues, "is not only different—but better. If evangelical leaders will take it seriously, it will make the church more like Jesus." You owe it to yourself to let Seel make his case even if you don't agree at every point. That goes double if you are a leader in the church. And if you are a parent or grandparent, *The New Copernicans* will help you better listen to and love the young adults in your life.

Denis Haack
Director, Ransom Fellowship
Editor, *Critique*

The New Copernicans is a thorough and prophetic education on human nature, sociology, and the future (or possible future) of the evangelical church. It is clear that John Seel has been listening carefully to a generation of millennials who right now do not feel at home in the evangelical church.

Greg Marshall
Chief Storyteller and Producer, CI Design, Inc.

The New Copernicans simply "gets it." Marketers, ministry leaders, parents, humanity: this is your codex to fundamentally unlearn and understand the spirit and journey of the modern mindset. We are living through a tipping point and this book contains the hopeful and corrective lantern to navigate this brave new world.

Phillip Colhouer
Director of Media and Cultural Engagement, Rio Vista Church

John Seel has made himself a student of millennials so the rest of us can learn. This book is sensitive without being pandering; it is empathetic without being mushy. Seel has written an anthropology for the world that's right in front of us but so often feels like foreign territory. I appreciate the hard-won wisdom of this book that refuses fear and traffics in hope.

James K. A. Smith
Professor of Philosophy, Calvin College
Author, *You Are What You Love* and *How (Not) to Be Secular*

John does a masterful job of outlining the cultural shift that is happening and the role of millennials in showing us (not causing) this shift. I found myself saying "Yes!" many, many times. I have experienced a deep spiritual hunger in our world, most notably at Burning Man, and John's *The New Copernicans* is an important resource if the church is going to sate that hunger.

The Very Rev. Dr. Brian Baker
Dean of the Trinity Cathedral, Sacramento, California

In an era of panoramic division, *The New Copernicans* is an essential bridge of understanding between worlds. John Seel articulates a generational frame shift with unique clarity, subtlety, and precision. This book is clearly a labor of love and the result is an opportunity for profound wisdom, healing, and transformation.

Jacob Marshall
Multisensory Artist and Aesthetic Philosopher
Cofounder, EMBC

I'm embarrassed to admit I have held an under-examined negative view of millennials. John has opened my eyes to what is possible, and particularly in the hands, minds, and souls of millennials themselves.

Tom Scott
Cofounder and CEO, The Nantucket Project

John Seel's *The New Copernicans* is a godsend. He makes the compelling case that the millennials can help us understand our cultural moment as well as our own faith. This insightful cultural analysis of the millennial generation and the modern evangelical church comes with a warning label: disregard at your own peril.

Frank A. James III, PhD, DPhil
President and Professor of Historical Theology,
Biblical Theological Seminary

In the world of narrative it is difficult to find people on a faith journey who talk the language of narrative. John Seel provides hope by giving insight into on-ramps that allow that process to begin. Plus, his footnotes give us a library of possibility.

Jack Hafer
Film Producer

In *The New Copernicans*, John Seel not only aptly diagnoses the challenge of engaging the millennial generation with the gospel but also tells the millennial story in its own terms, and with authenticity. This book describes an opportunity for churches to not only reach unreached people but, more importantly, to further embrace the ways of Jesus in their thinking and acting.

> Rev. Andy Hayball
> Executive Pastor, Trinity Church, Greenwich, Connecticut

Life is full of landmarks to be discovered. Great explorers find them, note them, and keep going forward learning by what they see and experience. They then tell others so they can see also. In *The New Copernicans* John Seel is a great explorer pointing out the landmarks of a new reality that is dawning and will touch every aspect of the church and life in general. John's insights paint the picture of a way forward in these turbulent times that are bursting with exploration and opportunity for those who have ears to hear.

> Dwight Gibson
> Chief Explorer
> The Exploration Group

Yes, yes, a thousand times, yes. That is how many exclamation points, check marks, and underlines accompany my reading of John Seel's *The New Copernicans*. He has clearly engaged in deep, pastoral listening in an effort to understand, affirm, and champion the next generation. This is theological sociology of the highest order. Utterly essential.

> Craig Detweiler
> Professor of Communication
> Pepperdine University

THE NEW COPERNICANS

THE NEW
COPERNICANS

MILLENNIALS
AND THE
SURVIVAL
OF THE CHURCH

DAVID JOHN SEEL, JR.

THOMAS NELSON
Since 1798

Published in Nashville, Tennessee, by Thomas Nelson. Thomas Nelson is a registered trademark of HarperCollins Christian Publishing, Inc.

Thomas Nelson titles may be purchased in bulk for educational, business, fund-raising, or sales promotional use. For information, please e-mail SpecialMarkets@ThomasNelson.com.

All Scripture quotations are taken from the Holy Bible, New International Version®, NIV®. Copyright © 1973, 1978, 1984, 2011 by Biblica, Inc.® Used by permission of Zondervan. All rights reserved worldwide. www.zondervan.com. The "NIV" and "New International Version" are trademarks registered in the United States Patent and Trademark Office by Biblica, Inc.®

Any Internet addresses, phone numbers, or company or product information printed in this book are offered as a resource and are not intended in any way to be or to imply an endorsement by Thomas Nelson, nor does Thomas Nelson vouch for the existence, content, or services of these sites, phone numbers, companies, or products beyond the life of this book.

ISBN 978-0-7180-9887-2 (softcover)
ISBN 978-0-7180-9888-9 (e-book)

Library of Congress Control Number: 2017946979

Printed in the United States of America
18 19 20 21 22 LSC 10 9 8 7 6 5 4 3 2 1

To Annie, David, and Alex,
the three millennials who shape my life

About Leadership✖Network

Leadership Network fosters innovation movements that activate the church to greater impact. We help shape the conversations and practices of pacesetter churches in North America and around the world. The Leadership Network mind-set identifies church leaders with forward-thinking ideas—and helps them to catalyze those ideas, resulting in movements that shape the church.

Together with HarperCollins Christian Publishing, the biggest name in Christian books, the NEXT imprint of Leadership Network moves ideas to implementation for leaders to take their ideas to form, substance, and reality. Placed in the hands of other church leaders, that reality begins spreading from one leader to the next . . . and to the next . . . and to the next, where that idea begins to flourish into a full-grown movement that creates a real, tangible impact in the world around it.

NEXT: A Leadership Network Resource
committed to helping you grow your next idea.

leadnet.org/NEXT

CONTENTS

CONTENTS

FOREWORD

In 1632 Galileo Galilei published a book on the two combating theories of the universe called *Dialogue Concerning the Two Chief World Systems*. The book takes the form of a dialogue, over the course of four days, between two main characters: Salviati, who represents the Copernican *heliocentric* view, in which the earth and the other planets orbit around the sun; and Simplicio, who represents the Ptolemaic/Aristotelian *geocentric* viewpoint, in which everything in the universe orbits around the earth. The book was not without controversy. In 1633 Galileo was brought to trial and found to be "vehemently suspect of heresy" and was placed under house arrest until his death nine years later. Galileo's book was placed on the *Index of Forbidden Books*, where it remained until 1835.

Galileo was a man caught between shadow and substance, in that liminal space where the world was changing. The established church held to a Ptolemaic view of the universe and they had the verses to prove it: "He set the earth on its foundations; / it can never be moved" (Ps. 104:5); and "The sun rises and the sun sets, and hurries back to where it rises" (Eccl. 1:5), for example. Yet what Galileo observed through his 20x power telescope told him a different story. It was the earth that moved.

Galileo was a Copernican caught in an Aristotelian age. Everything about his experience told him reality was different than what the established order was telling him. He was seeing the world through different lenses with different implications. He carefully brought facts and evidence to the bench, but old entrenched ideas, theories, and beliefs have a stickiness that is hard to displace. He couldn't find his place at the table.

Imagine what it was like for Galileo to realize through observation and experience that the world was *not* the way everyone else assumed it to be. Like Galileo, you, too, may be speaking the same language but think and experience something vastly different.

Today a new generation of Copernicans is emerging—those John Seel identifies as New Copernicans—who are experiencing and navigating life in a way that is different than their spiritual ancestors. This shift in frame is just as profound as going from a geocentric to a heliocentric view of the solar system. And like Copernicus, they are generally not taken seriously. The New Copernicans are modern explorers. Many are millennials, but other generations are part of this journey as well. New Copernicans have been shaped by Google (which puts the world's knowledge at their fingertips); social media platforms such as Instagram, Facebook, and Snapchat (through which they can tell their story to the world); exposure to cultural, racial, religious, and sexual diversity (which promotes a nonjudgmental approach to how others live their lives); on-demand entertainment (movies or church can be experienced anytime); as well as the disappointments and limitations of institutional *anything*—Wall Street, the Republican National Committee, the Democratic National Committee, businesses, the National Security Agency, and the church. New Copernicans don't view life in traditional binaries of sacred versus secular, biblical versus nonbiblical, left versus right, and so on. They are comfortable with both/and. They are the champions of non-dualistic unitive thinking. They don't place all their life experiences into clean categories or systems. Instead, they embrace a life lived off the edge of the map. They eschew our traditional maps and navigate by compass toward what is experientially good—good people, good experiences, good causes. It's a world where story trumps worldview; where experience trumps theology. Much has been written about the *whats* of millennials—what they want, what they like. Much has also been written about the *hows* of millennials—how to manage them, how to motivate them. John Seel helps us understand the *why* behind the whats and the hows. This book serves as a primer to introduce how an increasing number of people are thinking and experiencing life.

Disruptions don't look like much when they first happen, and the failure to see them comes not from a lack of intellect but from a failure of imagination. We can't imagine a time when the next generation won't step up and take their rightful place in the church. But the stubborn facts tell a different story. Millennials (born 1980 to 2000) comprise 23 percent of the United States population, but fewer than 10 percent of churches reflect this level of representation. According to a study of more than 4,400 churches by FaithCommunitiesToday.org, 18 percent of churches "report no young adult presence in their congregations."[1] According to Pew Research Center, 78 percent of "religious nones" were once active in church.[2] Another American church shutters its doors every 2.5

hours.[3] Churches thrive for a number of reasons but they close for one reason—a failure to reach the next generation. We are currently perfectly aligned to the results we are getting. If we want to get something different, we have to *think* something different and *do* something different. We'll need to experiment—even if that means trying over and over again—rather than ignoring the issue and continuing as we have.

The first Copernican, Galileo, knew he was right. Even after he was condemned for heresy, as he was led to prison, he is alleged to have muttered, "But the Earth still moves."[4] All the wisdom of Aristotle and Ptolemy, the authority of the established church, all the tradition of the status quo could not squelch this new reality. (With a touch of irony Galileo may have gotten the last laugh. In Florence's History of Science Museum, Galileo's middle finger sits alone in a small glass case atop a few astronomical instruments in defiance to all who thought him to be wrong.)[5]

Today the New Copernicans are here. They bring with them new ideas, new approaches, and new perspectives we have not considered or perhaps even heard before. As Apple Computer said about such pioneers in their advertising, "You can quote them, disagree with them, glorify or vilify them. About the only thing you can't do is ignore them."[6] We cannot dismiss them. We'll need to embrace a fresh humility that breathes, "For we know in part" (1 Cor. 13:9)—and ask for help from others on our common journey. I hope John Seel will be part of that journey for all of us.

—Eric Swanson

INTRODUCTION

THE TITANIC MISTAKE WE COULD MAKE

They received a warning, in fact nine warnings, but they were largely ignored. After the *RMS Titanic* received the iceberg alert, Captain Edward J. Smith made an incremental change in response, turning to a slightly southern course. Inexplicably, the ship maintained flank speed while posting a watch on the bow.

The Marconi radio operators in charge of passenger communications on the *Titanic* received even more updated and threatening warnings about icebergs, but as they were employed to facilitate passenger communication, they did not relay this information to the ship's bridge. Consequently, those with the greatest knowledge of the situation remained silent. Once an iceberg loomed directly ahead, there were few options still available. By then it was too late.

The disaster that followed cost more than 1,500 lives, including that of Captain Smith. It was the clumsy response to the impending collision that caused the sinking. A full-frontal direct hit of the iceberg might not have sunk the ship, though it would have done significant damage. Rather it was the last-minute panic and effort to avoid a collision that tore a hole through five compartments and doomed it. After the accident Captain Smith was a stoic hero in the best tradition of British seamanship: he went down with the ship. But it could have all been avoided.

It is widely acknowledged that hubris, not the iceberg, was the main culprit for the *Titanic's* sinking. The largest vessel at the time, she was equipped with the finest luxuries and latest technology, and deemed virtually unsinkable. When sailing an "unsinkable" ship on her maiden voyage, it is conceivable that her captain might ignore an unseen danger. It is the combination of invincibility and invisibility that creates the precondition for a crisis.

In radiotelephone communications, there are three levels of emergency radio warnings: *sécurité*, *pan-pan* (pronounced "pon-pon"), and *mayday*. These are professional ways of giving information in condensed verbal format—preceding an Urgency Marine Information Broadcast.

A pan-pan warning is an alert used by the Coast Guard over the marine radio to get mariners to pay attention. When a large cruise liner is leaving harbor, a military ship is entering harbor, or a ship carrying hazardous material is entering or leaving, mariners often receive a pan-pan alert on marine open channel 16. When there are potential hazards ahead a pan-pan warning is issued.

This book is a pan-pan alert.[1] There is a looming cultural frame shift, largely carried by millennials, which if ignored is poised to threaten the evangelical church. The warning is not limited to youth or college ministry, but encompasses the entire legacy and survivability of what is known as institutional evangelicalism.

While this book is focused on evangelicalism, mainline Protestant denominations and Roman Catholic churches are also facing the issues it raises. Not surprisingly, older divides between liberals and evangelicals and between Protestants and Catholics are not what they used to be. Being less either/or in orientation makes one more intrinsically ecumenical and should help us collectively reflect the wider body of Christ, the Apostles' Creed's "holy Catholic Church." This book is about the church wrestling with a significant cultural shift in perspective most often carried by its youngest members.

Everything will be touched by this shift. Those who adopt this new way of apprehending reality are the New Copernicans—the contemporary explorers of a new way of appropriating human society. What follows is a description of this New Copernican frame—what it is, what it means, and what difference it will make for the church. This New Copernican reality is the church's most pressing mission field.

The situation facing the evangelical church parallels that of the *Titanic* on that fateful April evening in 1912. The evangelical church has grown complacent, generally assured of ongoing growth by making comparisons with mainline or Catholic churches, which have experienced far more substantial decrease.[2] Coupled with this is a spiritual hubris that mixes American exceptionalism with an assumed spiritual vitality. However, it is becoming harder and harder to deny that evangelicalism is losing its hold on American culture. But because it has maintained such large market share for so long in the Bible Belt, it is easy to deny potential threats to its demise. The cultural dominance in the South and Midwest masks the increasing irrelevance of the church among those who curate the national social imaginary—the collective stories and myths we tell about the nature of reality and the shape of the good life. Coupled with the perennial confusion of politics with culture, this has left many with a false sense of optimism.

This is only compounded when evangelical leaders deny the importance of culture and cultural engagement. While culture may be invisible, it establishes the context for our beliefs and actions. It is of critical importance to the church to know how to read the "signs of the times."[3] Denying the reality of culture does not change it.

And finally, those closest to the problem, millennial pastors and youth ministers—like the Marconi radio operators on the *Titanic*—are the most aware of the pending crisis but are simultaneously disempowered to make a difference. Most senior church leadership does not take their perspectives seriously. What we are talking about here is not simply a leadership gap or a generation gap, but a perception gap. Millennial pastors and youth ministers might love to give greater voice to their own doubts and confusion, the kind of inherent messiness that attaches itself to belief today. But this kind of personal candor might not be well received by senior leadership. Consequently, they only talk openly with their peers via Facebook or Snapchat. It is easier to remain silent and avoid potential conflict.

It's unlikely that the evangelical church can survive if it is uniformly rejected by millennials—the coming generation of young adults—and so today the evangelical church faces a cross-generational crisis of enormous significance. A highly personal foretaste of the generational problem and impending institutional crisis within the church is seen in the strained relationships many evangelical leaders and pastors have with their millennial children. Many evangelical pastors' children have rejected the faith of their fathers and are best described as spiritually frustrated and homeless. We might be shocked to learn that 76 percent of those who are described by social scientists as religious nones or "religiously unaffiliated"—the fastest-growing segment of the American population—have a church background. The church itself is creating the growth of the unchurched. Close to 40 percent of millennials fit this religious profile.[4] Today roughly 80 percent of teens in evangelical church high school youth groups will abandon their faith after two years in college.[5] What we are doing to reach the next generation is *not* working: we are alienating our youth. There are relational examples of religious tension and abandonment in almost every evangelical family. This book seeks to explain why and further equip parents and church leaders in meeting these challenges.

Nonetheless, this is not a book merely about millennials, nor is it based on cohort analysis of the kind first made popular by Neil Howe and William Strauss, who coined the word *millennial*.[6] A cohort is a defined demographic grouping; cohort research assumes that a defined age group that shares common life experiences, particularly during their formative years, will create a distinctive perspective; that is, millennials will think differently because they all share similar life experiences from within a given time frame. This is *not* the point. Rather it is the acknowledgement that there is a fundamental frame shift in American society that is *carried,* not *caused,* by millennials—those born between 1980 and 2000—and this understanding of reality (or social imaginary) that they demonstrate is a direct challenge to the church. This shift in the social imaginary is more profound than can be solved by changing up marketing or ministerial tactics—it will require an entire paradigm shift across ministry.

This frame shift should not lead to spiritual hand-wringing. Instead, this New Copernican frame, this new way of processing reality, is not only different—but better. If evangelical leaders will take it seriously, it will make the church more like Jesus. Ironically, our millennial children are the greatest hope for the evangelical church to thrive and be salt and light in the midst of this tremendous cultural change.

Thus, the American evangelical church's response to this warning will either doom her or lead to a new awakening. Our millennial children, as well as nonchurchgoing millennials, are both the church's greatest challenge and its most exciting new opportunity. The difference will be in how we respond to this frame shift.

The New Copernicans is divided into six sections in twenty-six short chapters. This is a book of cultural analysis and is not an extended effort at providing a biblical rationale. However, as stated, I believe that the suggestions outlined here will enable the church to become more like Jesus. The research is heavily indebted to the work of Philadelphia philanthropist Sir John Templeton, Canadian philosopher Charles Taylor as mediated through Calvin College philosopher James K. A. Smith, British neuroscientist Iain McGilchrist, and British missiologist/theologian Lesslie Newbigin.[7]

Part 1 deals with the nature of this warning and suggests the prospects for the church if the warning is ignored. It also explains what we mean by a new frame—social imaginary in contrast to worldview—and a frame shift. It then suggests that a frame shift usually occurs not through reasoned argument but through the engagement of the imagination.

Part 2 outlines the contours of the coming frame shift—in effect it provides the location and outline of the iceberg. For obvious reasons, this is a crucial section. It describes the fundamental contrast between dwellers and explorers, between those with a closed versus open perspective. This is the essence of the shift in question.

Part 3 examines four current responses to this frame shift and what we can learn from each. Culture change does not happen in an instant; it is more of a process. Consequently, one can observe how even now people are dealing with this shift. There are four contemporary social imaginaries, and they will be contrasted with this new frame. Here we will discuss where there are growth opportunities for the church.

Part 4 examines more closely the way millennials see reality—their seven predominant characteristics—thereby providing greater clarity on the landscape of the emerging frame. Observing millennials gives us the chart for navigating the frame shift ahead. This section outlines priorities for the church if it is to reach millennials and respond effectively to the New Copernican frame.

Part 5 explores four on-ramps to this emerging frame—the shortcuts to success in walking in pilgrimage with New Copernicans. The church needs to become adept at navigating each on-ramp if it is to reach the entire spectrum of people, personality types, and spiritual searches represented by those who hold to this new perspective.

Part 6 explains why the coming generation of millennials is the hope of the church. Rather than hand-wringing over religious nones, we need to be celebrating the young advocates of this new frame. But it will mean listening and turning over responsibility to the emerging leadership of the millennial generation. In effect this is a call for the boomer generation to turn over the reins of the church to the emerging generation for the sake of the church. They are the harbor pilots best suited to navigate these waters. Years of past experience are no longer a benefit when one is entering uncharted waters.

This is a pan-pan warning, not a mayday-level crisis. There is still time for those with the will and openness to respond. We have all the information we need to see beyond the horizon. The only question is whether church leaders will have the foresight and humility to heed the warning and so maximize the opportunity for the church.

Here is where Captain Edward J. Smith failed. Mere confidence and momentum are not enough to avoid disaster. We need instead evangelical pastors and parachurch leaders who have a combination of courage and humility, as well as a heavy dose of imagination. We must not equate the kingdom of God with the status quo. We must not derive security from our past history, as was the repeated failure of the Israelites in the Old Testament. As an old man myself, I appeal to other old men and women to listen to our children, for it is our children who will be inheriting the world we now create. We must allow them the freedom to navigate the new frame and help direct the church through the emerging New Copernican social imaginary.

PART ONE

AN IGNORED WARNING

"To Titanic
    Ice report in lat 42.n to 41.25n Long 49w to long
50.30w saw much heavy pack ice and great number
of large icebergs·also field ice. Weather good clear."
    9:40 pm, Thursday, April 18, 1912
            FROM CLARKE, CAPTAIN MESABA[1]

The measure of leadership is best seen in times of crucial decision. Millennials carry a new frame on reality that poses a major challenge to the church in the coming years; this new frame is not only different, it is better. Like the iceberg warning to the Titanic, it should not be ignored. Through knowledge of this frame shift and all it entails, church leaders can learn how to navigate these uncharted waters. First we turn to examine what often cannot be seen—the importance of frames, how to navigate between them, and the cost if we do not.

ONE

SEEING WHILE NOT SEEING

You see what you expect to see. Depending on your frame, you can see and not see at the same time. When icebergs or cultural frame shifts are involved, this can be a problem.

In all our experiences, we think first in frames or in linguistic metaphors. C. S. Lewis observed, "All our truth, or all but a few fragments, is won by metaphor."[1] When we adopt a frame on reality, in effect all of reality is seen through that frame. George Lakoff, a professor of linguistics and cognitive science at Berkeley, writes, "People think in frames. . . . To be accepted, the truth must fit people's frames. If the facts do not fit the frame, the frame stays and facts bounce off."[2] Ideas do not stand alone. They come packaged in frames. And frames rule.

The traditional politicians and media pundits were shocked by the decision of the British people to leave the European Union. If they had paid attention to the public discourse—to the framing of the debate—the decision would have been less of a surprise. The choice before the British people was uniformly described in the public debate as "Brexit." In this description the entire choice was framed by the word *exit*. Again Lakoff observes, "When you are arguing against the other side: Do not use their language. Their language picks out a frame—and it won't be the frame you want."[3] The politicians who favored staying allowed the debate to be framed by leaving. In some ways they lost even before the vote by not paying sufficient attention to the framing of the debate.

The most powerful frames are those that shape our identity. Again it was observed that the Brexit vote was not based on facts about finances, but on emotions based on immigration. It was not decided on the basis of economics, but identity. Voters vote on the basis of who they are, what values they have, and who and what they admire. It is less a rational calculation than an emotional one. In the end Brexit was a vote to reclaim British identity. Frames are enormously important. And frame shifts should not be ignored.

We will be exploring a profound frame shift in the social imaginary. This shift is the invisible iceberg ahead, and the church is steaming toward it. Social imaginaries are different from worldviews and even more important. Charles Taylor writes,

By social imaginaries, I mean something much broader and deeper than intellectual schemes people may entertain when they think about social reality in a disengaged mode. I am thinking, rather, of the ways *people imagine their social existence* [Taylor's emphasis], how they fit together with others, how things go on between them and their fellows, the expectations that are normally met, and the deeper normative notions and images that underlie these expectations. . . . Because my focus is ordinary people, this is often carried in images, stories, and legends.[4]

Unlike worldviews, which tend to be more formal, academic, and cognitive (falling under various "isms": theism, deism, naturalism, pantheism), social imaginaries are our unthinking assumptions about the nature of the good life embedded in our commercial brands and sense of self. Abercrombie & Fitch, Victoria's Secret, and True Religion are selling more than cloth. They are selling a story that is tacitly embraced by those who wear their products.[5] Abercrombie "is arguably more blatantly in-your-face about sex and body image than any other brand marketed to teenagers in the history of retail"—and has gotten into hot water recently not for its sex, but its priority on thin models.[6] Social imaginaries are more about the stories we tell in our advertising and movies than the philosophies we articulate in a classroom or in a book.

Millennials are *carriers, not the cause,* of a fundamental and lasting shift in the social imaginary in American society. The dominant culture is telling a different story about the nature of the good life from that of the traditional evangelical church. Out of the four concurrent social imaginaries in American society that I will discuss, one in particular is dominated by the curators of the public social imaginary—the storytelling cultural creatives—and is therefore the most influential. Furthermore, two of the four social imaginaries or frames are becoming increasingly passé, one of which is unfortunately dominated by the evangelical church.

There is one additional point to make about frames. Reason and rational argument work effectively within a frame, but they are ineffective between frames. For instance, if the frame of sex is merely a pleasurable activity between two consenting adults, then the biblical fact "Marriage should be honored by all, and the marriage bed kept pure" (Heb. 13:4) will make no sense in that frame. In today's world, before we talk about sexual facts, we need to talk about sexual frames—we need to reimagine sexuality first. Few within or without the church immediately connect sexuality with spirituality (more on this in chapter 23). The confusion is a matter of frames, not a matter of facts. Moving between frames happens through engaging the imagination or through lived experience. A frame shift, like all paradigm shifts, is the result of a transrational aha moment that results in thinking outside the box or outside the given frame. Reason works within frames, the imagination between them. Piling on facts when they don't fit the frame will change nothing. Instead one needs a new story.

Since the American evangelical church is heavily committed to rational left-brained Enlightenment ways of thinking and the apologetic approaches that reinforce it, the church and its leaders are temperamentally crippled in their ability to see or accept a frame shift. We are weakest in the very ways of thinking in which frames are shifted. The American evangelical church has an underdeveloped poetic imagination—in fact, it is sometimes viewed with outright suspicion.[7] The imagination is viewed as subjective and therefore intrinsically relativistic. This is not only bad theology, but bad neuroscience.[8] The point here is simply that our bias toward rational left-brained Enlightenment thinking makes it very hard for the evangelical church to communicate effectively to a cultural frame shift.

This attitude makes it very hard for many leaders within institutional evangelicalism to heed the warning of the coming frame shift in the social imaginary. They see and don't see at the same time. For some it will take an impending institutional collapse before they will attend to the warnings that could have helped them avoid much of the looming crisis—losing the future generations that are crucial for the church's survival.

Just as the politicians and pundits missed the changing sensibility of the British people about the European Union, so evangelical leaders remain largely unaware of the shifting frames of young people and what this portends for the church. This blindness will leave many evangelical institutions—colleges, seminaries, and parachurch organizations—in a position of panic and paralysis.

But there is still time to put on the 3-D glasses that allow this story to come into focus. Remember, this is a pan-pan warning, not a mayday call. It is a timely warning, not an immediate crisis.

The way to observe the contours of this shift is to examine millennials. As the inchoate carriers of this shift in the social imaginary, examining their attitudes and behaviors becomes an efficient and effective way of observing these patterns in real life. We don't need to start with abstractions or survey instruments, as both have a way of creating distractions and distortions. If we listen to millennials and walk with them without judgment, the contours of the new social landscape they are creating will emerge. Let's explore how our traditional frames have served to distort our understanding of millennials.

TAKEAWAYS FROM CHAPTER ONE

- Frames dictate what we see and don't see.
- When the facts don't fit the frame, the facts bounce off and the frame stays.
- Social imaginaries are the stories we tell about the good life.
- Social imaginaries are the most important frame because they shape our identity and are largely unconscious.
- Reason works within frames, imagination between them.

DISCUSSION QUESTIONS FOR CHAPTER ONE

- What is the significance of frames?
- What is a social imaginary? Can you think of examples from recent books or films that get at what is the good life? Consider, for example, recent Oscar-nominated films.
- Do you agree with the weaknesses in the evangelical church that the chapter points out? Why or why not?

TWO

GETTING THINGS IN FOCUS

Frames dictate our view of reality. They both clarify and obscure. We see some things more clearly and other things not at all. Thomas Kuhn, famous for his work on scientific paradigm shifts, notes, "What a man sees depends both upon what he looks at and also upon what his previous visual-conceptual experience has taught him to see."[1] As we have discussed, reason works well within frames, but it is almost useless between them. Frame shifts do not happen because of a greater application of reason. They happen when the imagination is able to picture reality in a new way—through a new frame. The greatest scientific breakthroughs happened in exactly this manner.

It was the imagination, not reason, that led Einstein to his insights on relativity. His biographer Walter Isaacson observes, "As a theorist, his success came not from the brute strength of his mental processing but from his imagination and creativity."[2] Einstein's theories of relativity did not develop from the further application of experimental data; first it was a picture, a thought experiment of the imagination, when as a sixteen-year-old boy he imagined what it would be like to ride alongside a light beam. Einstein declared, "Imagination is more important than knowledge."[3]

So, too, was the experience of astronomer Nicolaus Copernicus, who in the spring of 1543 lay on his deathbed in Frombork, Poland. He was seventy-one years old. His followers brought him the first printed copy of his life's work, *On the Revolutions of Celestial Orbits,* straight from the press. Copernicus died that same day.

His book launched the scientific revolution, but didn't produce a paradigm shift in thought until a century and a half later, when Isaac Newton published his *Mathematical Principles of Natural Philosophy* in 1687. Copernicus didn't have a theory in mind when he postulated his view of planetary motion; rather he had a "flash of insight," a new picture in mind.[4] His challenge of the Ptolemaic geocentric universe is the exemplar of a scientific paradigm shift. These shifts do not happen by the application of more facts and data, but by a shift in the "visual gestalt" or through a new frame or paradigm.[5]

The frame shift being carried by millennials is potentially as groundbreaking and world changing as Copernicus's discovery was. New Copernicans are the explorers of a new frame on reality. Grasping their new way of perceiving reality will require a leap of the imagination, perhaps especially for older readers.

What we learn from the academic study of scientific paradigm shifts is that "when paradigms change, there are usually significant shifts in the criteria determining the legitimacy of problems and of proposed solutions,"[6] according to Kuhn. To put it another way, when the game changes from Hearts to Spades, what is deemed to be trump also changes. And if you think we're playing Hearts when the game is Spades, you will soon be left holding a losing hand.

Thus it's important to know what is now trump in a millennial-driven New Copernican world.

The content of the frame we are considering is the social imaginary. Consequently, the curators of the national social imaginary, the storytelling cultural creatives—songwriters, filmmakers, and advertisers—play a significant role in defining reality or outlining the contours of the social imaginary for most people. They establish and legitimize the assumptions most people make about their lives. Evangelicals are largely underrepresented among these national cultural gatekeepers. We are not in this conversation, and even if we were included, we are not speaking in a manner that makes sense to them.

So not only are evangelicals structurally removed from national circles of storytelling influence, evangelicalism has a consistent bias against the imagination—the very conceptual tool needed to accept a frame shift. Many evangelical leaders will resist the warning. This puts institutional evangelicalism at risk.

However, we are already seeing the consequences of not making the leap to understand the New Copernican frame. The power of frames explains why so much of the research done on millennials is distorted. Most millennials resist being called millennials because the national narrative on them is so pejorative, patronizing, and just wrong. If you are telling a story about a generational cohort and they can't see themselves in the story you are telling and, worse, are offended by the story, then it's pretty evident there is something fundamentally wrong with the story you are telling. This is how most millennials feel.

Moreover, the litany of stereotypes used to describe millennials makes it nearly impossible to appreciate their positive insights. The typical descriptors are entitled, sheltered, tech-obsessed, and too sensitive.[7] The ABC sitcom *The Great Indoors* builds its humor on these unfair characteristics. In doing so, it is a generational put-down. It is not surprising that when this show debuted at the Television Critics Association gathering in the summer of 2016, millennial reporters howled in protest.[8] The show's producers only thought it further proved their point: "people saying their feelings were hurt for being depicted as too sensitive."[9] While most stereotypes about millennials have a modicum of truth, here they create a negative bias that blinds us to their valuable contribution.

Often millennial researchers are trying to describe a 3-D reality through a 2-D lens, as Edwin Abbott depicted in his 1884 novella, *Flatland*.[10] They see something, but their perspective is off. Most millennial research has been framed in categories rejected by millennials. It has been observed that "You can't solve a problem within the same frame that created it." If we ask boomer-framed questions of millennials, we'll get an answer, but the survey answers will be distorted because the survey instrument will not be asking the questions within a millennial frame. To get a genuine millennial perspective, the questions themselves would have to fit within a millennial frame.[11]

Consider two ads that target millennials. The first is from State Farm. Like all insurance companies, State Farm sells risk abatement against an anticipated life trajectory. Their ad "Never" assumes an ongoing generational continuity between millennials and boomers, even if somewhat delayed.[12] It illustrates the "maturational delay" explanation referred to by Pew researchers. The male character in the ad pronounces, "I'm never getting married. I'm never having children. I'm never moving to the suburbs. I'm never going to drive a minivan. I'm never having more children," while going on to do precisely those things. This ad is based on the faulty assumption that millennials will eventually age to look just like their parents, that what is at play in their distinctiveness is nothing more than being slow to mature. This is an analysis that favors the status quo; it assumes that millennials will resort back to the older frame as they age, when in fact this is highly unlikely. This ad avoids considering millennials as representing a fundamental and lasting frame shift. And in line with unfair stereotypes, it also paints them as being full of themselves and resistant to the old frame's idea of the good life due to laziness and other character flaws.

The second ad is from Lincoln MKC, Ford Motor Company's luxury brand, and features actor Matthew McConaughey.[13] Driving in the desert, McConaughey explains in his distinctive drawl, "I've been driving Lincolns long before anyone paid me to drive one. I didn't do it to be cool, didn't do it to make a statement. I just liked it." Developed by the New York ad agency Hudson Rouge, this spot successfully captures millennials' high regard for authenticity, expressive individualism, and experience. *International Business Times* notes, "Lincoln, according to *AdAge*, has contracted McConaughey to win a 'younger, more progressive' consumer. The TV ad you've probably seen by now is just the beginning: The deal is multiyear and will include digital spots created by Danish director Nicolas Winding Refn that attempt to get viewers to experience the MKC through 'unscripted moments' [read *authentic*] with McConaughey."[14] Sales for Lincoln have risen 25 percent since the ad series began. The grounding rationale for life's choices according to this ad is simply "I just liked it." This agency understands millennials. Careful analysis can save companies from missing the mark with this substantial, hype-proof, media-savvy, brand-defining audience. We will be looking at the seven positive characteristics of millennials later. If the church gets this wrong, it will be to its own substantial loss.

Millennials have been the subject of extensive market and survey research. Again, the results of this research are dependent on the questions asked and the frame through which the results are interpreted. Pew researchers tell us the three frames through which they analyze their survey results on millennials: (1) delayed maturation, (2) low social capital, and (3) decreased religious affiliation.[15] These three frames do not emerge from listening to millennials, but are sociological theories being overlaid on the data.

If we are to see clearly, we must not allow ourselves to fall into these traps of interpreting millennials through the old frame. It is unlikely that we would arrive at these insights on our own without listening to what millennials say about themselves. We are in their debt. They can help us see clearly and get back in focus. For we have much to learn from them: as we will discuss, not only do New Copernicans see things differently, they actually see things better—better in the sense that it will make us more like Jesus.

Nowhere is the distorting perception and bias of the old frame seen more clearly than in the evangelical church's proclivity for left-brain thinking.

TAKEAWAYS FROM CHAPTER TWO

- Imagination, not reason, often leads to scientific breakthroughs.
- Carriers of this frame shift are largely millennials, those I call New Copernicans.
- Frames explain the reason so much of the research done on millennials is distorted.
- Pejorative stereotypes blind us to the insights and contributions of millennials.

DISCUSSION QUESTIONS FOR CHAPTER TWO

- How are frames shifted?
- Why are spiritually oriented millennials called New Copernicans?
- Why is research on millennials so consistently distorted? Do you agree?
- What negative stereotypes of millennials have you experienced? What stereotypes are most wrong?

THREE

LEFT-BRAIN THINKING

ESCAPING THE HALL OF MIRRORS

There are two different ways of approaching reality—consider the examination of a rabbit. Who has a better understanding of a rabbit: the *scientist* who dissects the rabbit on his lab table and writes a thesis on its anatomy, physiology, embryology, biochemistry, and so on or the *artist*, like Albrecht Dürer, who paints with intellectual sympathy and captures all that is inexpressibly in the rabbit? The scientist sees the rabbit in parts, in factual fragments. The artist sees the rabbit whole and captures its essence with a childlike comprehension that approaches love. One is knowledge by disassembly, the other knowledge by union. German philosopher Wilhelm Dilthey, championing the importance of the intuitive mind, writes, "Poetry protects, as it were, all that which can be experienced but not explained so that it will not vanish under the dissecting operations of an abstract science."[1] He assumes that something precious is lost when an embodied experience is put in abstract categories.

Love is not a mathematical formula and a sunset not a paint-by-number canvas. There are some experiences that defy explanation and formula, where silence and wonder are a better response.

The intuitive and the analytical ways of knowing are roughly reflected in the right and left hemispheres of the brain. According to neuroscience, the brain hemispheres are designed to work collaboratively, with the analytical mind subservient to the intuitive, the left to the right. As an example of this order, neuroscientist Iain McGilchrist argues that language is derived from music and not the other way around. He writes, "If it should turn out that music leads to language, rather than language to music, it helps us understand for the first time the otherwise baffling historical fact that poetry evolved before prose."[2] But things have gotten out of sorts in the past three hundred years. The West now is biased toward the left hemisphere of the brain to the exclusion of the right.

McGilchrist argues that in the West since the Enlightenment there has been usurpation, a reversal, and subsequent domination of the left brain over the right; and all this is to our loss. This process has meant that we are increasingly trapped in a hall of mirrors, trapped in abstractions of our own making, unable to comprehend or connect with actual embodied reality. We now accept a perspective about reality that is theoretical, abstract, fragmented, and hegemonic—demanding its own way. One does not have to look any further than any seminary systematic theology textbook to see this. We've adopted a reductionist frame of reference that keeps us from seeing or experiencing the real.[3] Yet it is a perspective that seems for most people totally normal.[4] We are conceptually blind, while we think we are seeing. We know facts but have no sense of their meaning. We get the what, but never the why: discrete facts, but not whole context. We swim with sharks, but never ask if we are lunch.

McGilchrist believes that the universe is built on a plan and that the inner structure of our brains reflects the structure of the universe. Not only does our brain "dictate the shape of the experience we have of the world," but "it reflects in its structure and functioning, the nature of the universe."[5]

Millennials get this. They have come to reject the distorting way we are using our brains, the left-brain bias. This is why they always prioritize lived experience over abstract reflection. Much of our pedagogy is head, heart, and hand, or observation, interpretation, and application, when just the reverse is actually how we learn: hand, heart, and then head. The import of this neurological insight for our analysis is that millennials not only think differently, they think better. They have intuited a more accurate assessment of human nature and reality. Bob Sample observed, "Albert Einstein called the intuitive or metaphoric mind a sacred gift. He added that the rational mind was a faithful servant. It is paradoxical that in the context of modern life we have begun to worship the servant and defile the divine."[6] So our goal in attending to millennials is not to beef up our youth or college ministry; it is not to better accommodate our sensibilities to culture so as to be more hip or relevant. No, we listen to millennials because this frame shift they have adopted is a corrective to three hundred years of distorted thinking, a corrective to our own blindness.

This frame shift is not based on highly speculative cohort research—a kind of research that should be generally taken with a grain of salt—but on cutting-edge neuroscience. Not surprisingly, this neuroscience research serves to reinforce the biblical.[7] As we will see, this millennial frame shift will lead us to a more thoroughly biblical stance toward life and reality: a way of apprehending the world that is more Trinitarian, incarnational, communal, mystical, and aspirational.

So much for lamenting millennials—they are instead the hidden treasure of the church. It's important that we approach this book and millennials not as a quest for relevance or marketing savvy, but as a portal for a more accurate assessment on human nature and reality. Millennials have insights from which we have much to gain. And millennials will have much to learn from us to regain confidence in the church. Parents have much to learn from their millennial children. It is high time that we listen carefully and listen well.

Millennials came to these insights not because they read books on philosophy, history, neuroscience, or sociology, but because the culture in which they grew up has largely abandoned the foundations on which modernity was formed. Consequently, millennials represent the first post-Enlightenment, postmodern generational cohort. Let's examine what it is they are rejecting.

THE ENLIGHTENMENT PROJECT

The Enlightenment was a philosophical movement that emerged in the eighteenth century—around the time of the American and French Revolutions. It was largely a rejection of the medieval synthesis and gave rise to a celebration of science, reason, and technology.[8] The Reformation in the sixteenth century and the Wars of Religion in the seventeenth century were instrumental in contributing to the breakup of the medieval synthesis. From this emerged in time our modern world, the world we describe as modernity.

The dynamics of these cultural transformations are complex and multifaceted. They are not merely the fruit of intellectual history—a few great minds and a few important books—but are the conjunction of economic and political forces that led to the realignment of power and influence among ruling elites. It is a complex story that transpired over several centuries.[9]

For our purposes, it's important to note that there has long been established collaboration between Protestants and the Enlightenment. Missiologist Lesslie Newbigin writes, "During the worldwide explosion of European political, commercial, and military power following the Enlightenment, Christian missions shared in this expansion. Christian missions were, in fact, among the main carriers of the ideas of the Enlightenment into the other continents. . . . The churches of Europe and their cultural offshoots in the Americas had largely come to a kind of comfortable cohabitation with the Enlightenment."[10] Protestant churches were the global standard bearers of the Enlightenment. This means that the millennial abandonment of the Enlightenment will heavily impact contemporary evangelicalism. Evangelicalism and the Enlightenment share many common characteristics; one cannot reject one without doing significant damage to the other.

As noted previously, Iain McGilchrist suggests that since the Enlightenment, the West has distorted the way the brain is supposed to work and thereby adopted a distorted view of reality. This distortion is intrinsic to much of evangelical thinking. He poses this question: "Let us try to imagine what the world would look like if the left hemisphere became so far dominant that, at the phenomenological level, it managed more or less to suppress the right hemisphere's world altogether."[11] These are the tendencies he sees in Western society and which millennials see in the evangelical church.

It would be a world where there is the loss of the broader picture in favor of a detailed, fragmented view of the world. Specialization and technical knowledge would triumph. This kind of abstract information would take precedence over knowledge that comes from experience. Eventually the theoretical or abstract would seem to be more convincing than concrete experience. But this is backwards.

These are realities reflected in some of the tensions felt in seminary education between systematic and biblical theology, and between academic and pastoral theology. For example, when talking about Job's anger at God and the benefits of this kind of anger in our discipleship, the more academic and abstract theologian will feel the need to parse out different kinds of anger and ascertain whether each are actually theologically correct. Here abstract theological correctness has to have the last word over the messiness of lived experience, which was Job's point. These kinds of theologians cannot simply live with the messiness of anger directed at God from the acute pain of lived existence—even when it borders on sin. Try this kind of careful parsing of anger with a struggling millennial and the theologian is apt to get his middle finger. Likewise, Job's friends were uniformly not helpful.

This is the world described by Michael Lewis in his book *The Big Short*. The financial crisis of 2007–2008 is an example of reality catching up to an abstract world of collateralized debt obligations and those who had the prescience to short the market.[12] Together these men make a fortune by taking advantage of the impending economic collapse in America. The debt instruments—the collateralized debt obligations (CDO)—were not backed by reality. This is a world where no one was dealing with cash or even actual mortgages, but abstracted instruments of debt on a computer screen with little to no actual relationship to reality. It was a bubble born of a mind-set where abstractions became reality.

Of this left-brain–oriented world, McGilchrist writes, "The world as a whole would become more virtualized, and our experience of it would be increasingly through meta-representations of one kind or another; fewer people would find themselves doing work involving contact with anything in the real, 'lived' world, rather than with plans, strategies, paperwork, management, and bureaucratic procedures."[13] In this world, numbers replace faces, the impersonal for the personal, and the virtual for real life. McGilchrist expands on this: "'Either/or' would tend to be substituted for matters of degree, and a certain inflexibility would result."[14] The priority in such a world is control. Religion would be discounted as mere fantasy. While the world has not fully succumbed to this rationalized world, its expanding tendencies are all around us. It is these tendencies that millennials reject in their abandonment of the Enlightenment project.

Consider the way in which we have been taught to study the Scriptures: observation, interpretation, and application, or head, heart, and hand. This is a thoroughly modernist approach to Bible study. The evangelical church has adopted an "intellectualist model of education," as evidenced by the evangelical church's preoccupation with the worldview approach to apologetics and discipleship.[15] Millennials and the best of neuroscience would tell us that we've gotten it just backwards. We learn best from experience that captures our imagination and which we subsequently reflect upon analytically: hand, heart, and head. Millennials assume experiential learning that is the opposite of Enlightenment assumptions: where embodiment takes precedence over cognition, practice over principle, street over book smarts, and lived experience over classroom theory. Theirs is a post-Enlightenment perspective where the messiness of an incarnational reality is paramount.

There are some who see in this a return to the 1960s, reminiscent of the romanticism of the hippies. This would be a mistake and is a backhanded way of discounting the frame shift we are witnessing. It is best not to take a flippant been-there-done-that attitude toward the current millennial frame shift. It is profound, culture shaping, and not likely to change. We now live between the lightning and the thunder, between the flash of insight and sound of all traditional institutions being completely reshaped—not the least of which will be the church. Millennials are poised to change our understanding of human society. Their perspective potentially overturns three hundred years of institutionalized assumptions—many of which are embedded in the evangelical church.

To confirm this shift, most of us do not have to look any further than our own children. Many have consciously walked away from this hall of mirrors.

TAKEAWAYS FROM CHAPTER THREE

- There are two distinct approaches to reality: the intuitive mind and the analytical mind.
- For the past three hundred years, the left brain—the analytical mind—has usurped the role of the right brain and thereby distorted our understanding of reality.
- The inner structure of the brain points to the design for how we are to understand reality. Neuroscience points to a corrective to this error.
- New Copernicans reject this three-hundred-year-old left-brain analytical bias.
- New Copernicans are thus the first post-Enlightenment generational cohort.
- The evangelical church is heavily aligned with this Enlightenment thinking to its own loss, as evangelicals are

increasingly disconnected from reality, living instead in a hall of mirrors.

DISCUSSION QUESTIONS FOR CHAPTER THREE

- How are the two hemispheres of the brain supposed to work together?
- How have you seen Enlightenment thinking play out in your own life, community, or church?
- Why has this made millennials more attracted to the more liturgical church traditions?
- What community is most oriented to the intuitive mind? What role do they have within the evangelical church?

FOUR

FUGITIVES IN THE PEW

Discussions of acute social change and pan-pan warnings of a cultural frame shift are disorienting to people of an older generation. Yet they come into focus when they consider the lives and perspectives of their children and grandchildren. Many evangelical parents are well aware of the challenges of transferring their faith to the next generation. Many of their children are in various forms of disengagement with the church and their parents' beliefs. You may find this book valuable only in that it helps you understand your own children and gives advice on how you can assist them on their ongoing spiritual pilgrimages—and that's a good value.

Church leaders are well aware that the future of the evangelical church in America is closely tied to reaching millennials. They are now the largest demographic cohort in America and the most influential in terms of commercial brand success. The church cannot hope to survive without grappling with reaching millennials.

Researchers refer to those who reached adulthood around 2000 as millennials. Currently, they are the largest single grouping

of Americans and the most powerful consumer group with pur-
chasing power that will exceed boomers' this year—approximately
$1.3 trillion in direct spending.[1] At 23.4 percent of the American
population, millennials are 75.4 million strong.[2] Compounding
their influence, this generation will receive a thirty trillion–dollar
wealth transfer from boomers over the next twenty years.[3] Because
of this, they have been the subjects of extensive market research.
Not only are they economically significant, but culturally and religiously as well.[4]

However, there is a subset of this generation that bears special
attention: the millennial children of churchgoing evangelical parents. These children feel trapped. David Kinnaman, president of
Barna Group and bestselling author, describes them as nomads,
people who have a mix of positive and negative feelings about their
faith. Most are disenchanted with religion but have not cut all ties
to their faith or to their church.[5] They have one foot in and one foot
out. Perhaps a better word than *nomad*, which suggests their freedom to drift from their faith, would be *fugitives*. They are trapped,
stuck, imprisoned—conceptual slaves. Typically they have not been
given the freedom to express their confusion and frustration out
loud. Institutions that assume true faith and correct thinking are
two sides of the same coin are not usually safe places to express
doubt. When belief and doubt are binary rather than a fused experience—as preferred by New Copernicans—the stakes are too high
to be honest about doubt.[6] The church is not a safe place to voice
confusion. Consequently, many independent-thinking teens keep
these doubts and disenchantments bottled up until college. Under
these intellectual, emotional, and spiritual conditions, it is hardly
surprising that close to 80 percent of children who participated in
high school church youth programs abandon their faith during

college.[7] We have created conditions that leave many of these children spiritually frustrated and eventually homeless. By failing to understand this frame shift we are literally pushing them away from the church. Almost a quarter of Americans now claim no religious affiliation, those researchers describe as religious nones.[8] According to a study by Public Religion Research Institute, "the religiously unaffiliated now outnumber Catholics, white mainline Protestants, and white evangelical Protestants, and their growth has been a key factor in the transformation of the country over the last decade from a majority white Christian nation to a minority white Christian nation."[9] These children of well-meaning and faithful evangelical parents frequently have no on-ramps to a more thoughtful and humane expression of faith. They cannot give doubt a voice. In short, our ignorance—and perhaps arrogance—is turning their doubt into skepticism, their fugitive status toward being prodigals, their antipathy toward atheism. We need to stop pushing them out of the pew.

If we would listen and understand, if we would engage on the basis of a comprehension of this frame shift, if we would respect where they are in their confused spiritual journey, if we would agree to simply walk with them, then an angry atheism or prodigal status in college is not a foregone conclusion.

As the headmaster of a Christ-centered classical college prep school, I was well aware that there were always a handful of students enrolled in my school that did not want to be there, but were forced to attend by their well-meaning parents. At the outset of my tenure as headmaster, I spent two weeks speaking to every student in the school for ten to fifteen minutes, trying to ferret out these students. "Do you really want to be here?" I would ask.

One student, whose dress, tattoos, and piercings clearly marked him as an outlier to the spit-and-polished image of a Christian school student, came clean: "Dr. Seel," he said, looking at the floor, "I don't want to be here. I feel trapped. My mom is on the school board, and this is the last place I want to attend school."

My response startled him. "Bobby, it's your life and your faith. You need to stop complaining about your parents and take charge of your own life. If you want to get out of here, it's not a hard concept. Bring twenty-five dollars' worth of marijuana to school and you are history. But you've got to stop playing the victim." He was edgy and I gave him edgy back. Because I treated him like an adult and took his grievances seriously he stayed, came around, and graduated with honors.

We have got to find a way to enter into relationships with those who feel like they are fugitives in the pew. There are more on-ramps to a more thoughtful and humane faith than they have known— social justice, nature, beauty, and loving relationships.[10] These will be explored further later in this book. Many of these on-ramps will need to be couched in lived experiences outside the institutional church. We need to move past their religious defenses to get them to explore honestly a spiritual path, which may lead them to Jesus.

The fugitives in the pew need us to start listening closely, respecting their confusion, and walking with them there, without feeling the need to provide a litany of answers and quick-and-easy solutions. The answers will come in the experience of walking in pilgrimage together in a shared spiritual adventure—coparticipants in a spiritual exploration during which we learn from one another. It is particularly important for parents to think of faith as a pilgrimage rather than a light switch; a movie rather than a snapshot.

The important thing is to get our children out of this feeling of being trapped—either by not respecting their agency or by dictating narrow theological boxes for them to live in. Of course, there are risks in an open pilgrimage, but it is the only way to genuinely find an authentic relationship with Jesus. Clearly what the church is doing is not working, as there is a continual drift away from the church by the younger generation.

TAKEAWAYS FROM CHAPTER FOUR

- The future of the evangelical church is closely tied to its ability to reach the millennial generation.
- Millennials (born between 1980 and 2000) are now the largest single demographic cohort in America. Their influence in society cannot be overstated.
- Millennial children of evangelical parents—hybrid New Copernicans—are at great spiritual risk, best described as fugitives, feeling trapped and restless.
- We need to be able to give our millennial children an on-ramp to a more thoughtful, humane expression of genuine Christian faith.

DISCUSSION QUESTIONS FOR CHAPTER FOUR

- What is your personal experience with millennials?
- If you have millennial children, what is their spiritual trajectory?
- What steps have you taken to provide them with an on-ramp to a genuine relationship with Jesus?

FIVE

VOTING WITH ONE'S FEET

Some warnings are jarring and immediate. "Mayday," for example. Most, however, are subtle and incremental, like a pan-pan warning: "Pay attention." These are the most common and also the most dangerous because they can be ignored.

A complete blockage of a major heart artery can cause a person to drop like a rock. We've all been told the signs: nausea, tingling in the left arm, and a crushing, elephant-like weight on the chest. When the signs are this severe, there is little that can be done medically unless that person happens to drop on the floor of a hospital's emergency room. Receiving CPR within three minutes, defibrillation within eight minutes—if you are not young or have a low body temperature (as in the EMS throwaway observation, "You are not dead until you are warm and dead")—is the standard best-case scenario for reviving a stopped heart.

Most of the time the signs are less severe. In these cases the pain one might feel from the lack of oxygen to the heart muscle is no more painful than the last rep in a series of dumbbell curls. Most macho men can push through it. Herein lies the problem: *a failure to attend to the incremental signs, when steps can still be taken, can lead to a big crisis.*

This was my experience. I had a heart attack while on a casual daily walk. It felt no more painful than a summer brain freeze from an icy drink. Nothing more. I went a week before doing anything about it. Yes, it has a medical name: crescendo angina. When I mentioned it to my sister, who is a medical doctor, after looking up the symptoms on the Internet a week later, she said to go immediately to the hospital. I was giving a speech in an hour and debating going after the speech. I hated to abandon them at the last minute. Such is the danger of not attending to small signs.

One wonders when the evangelical church will attend to their pending generational crisis. The church is in decline, but we reason that our 2 percent drop is not nearly as bad as the 10 percent drop facing Catholics. We'd do well to remember acclaimed sociologist Peter Berger's warning, "The key characteristic of all pluralistic situations is that the religious ex-monopolies can no longer take for granted the allegiance of their client populations."[1] Our dominance and monopoly status is not a given.

But when we focus on young people—particularly millennials— the numbers tell a much more alarming story. Nearly 40 percent of young adults (ages 18 to 29) are religiously unaffiliated. This is a fourfold increase from young adults a generation ago. In 1986, for example, only 10 percent of young adults claimed no religious affiliation. This means that more young people identify as unaffiliated than identify with all forms of Protestantism combined. Today 25 percent of Americans claim no formal religious identity, making them the largest single "religious group" in the United States.[2] The church is potentially one generation away from extinction. Of those who have left the church, the majority made this decision while in high school and most because they simply stopped believing in the religion's teachings.

We're unlikely to see visible antireligious marching in the streets. Millennials remain close to their parents, as many are still living at home. What we will see is a quiet drifting away. Theirs is a passive-aggressive rebellion—more in line with crescendo angina. And these trends are likely to accelerate in the coming years as a majority (54 percent) of unaffiliated Americans are marrying people with their same religious orientation. About 70 percent of those raised in unaffiliated religious households maintain their lack of religious identity into adulthood. We cannot count on them returning to the church as they mature.

Viewing youth and religion through this framework obscures as much as it reveals. Do not think that the religiously unaffiliated are atheists or agnostics. Even as they drift away from religious institutions, many still attend spiritual events, pray, and believe in God. When approached correctly with the right attitude and tone, there remains an enormous, perhaps even unprecedented, opportunity for spiritual advancement among this age group.[3]

So this pan-pan warning deserves our immediate attention. Culture is changing and the window of opportunity for a meaningful response by the American evangelical church is closing. Minimally, we should pay close attention to those areas of our nation where these trends are most prevalent—Portland and Seattle, Austin and Madison, New York and Los Angeles. What is now a visible trickle may soon become an irreversible torrent. We are on the cusp of losing the coming generation and the institutions that are dependent on their continued involvement, such as Christian colleges and universities. Sociologist Peter Berger warns,

The pluralistic situation presents the religious institutions with two ideal-typical options. They can accommodate themselves to the situation, play the pluralistic game of religious free enterprise, and come to terms as best they can with the plausibility problem by modifying their product in accordance with consumer demands. Or they can refuse to accommodate themselves, entrench themselves behind whatever socio-religious structures they can maintain or construct, and continue to profess the old objectivities as much as possible as if nothing had happened.[4]

The evangelical church is not alone in facing this generational challenge. A similar challenge faces the International Olympic Committee. The most recent numbers from the Rio Olympics show that there has been a 30 percent drop in TV viewers between the ages of 18 and 34. In response five new games were added to the Tokyo 2020 Olympics: sport climbing, surfing, skateboarding, karate, and baseball/softball. But even this was met with millennial resistance. More than seven thousand skateboarders signed a petition asking the IOC not to include skateboarding in the Olympics fearing that it would be co-opted by global commercial interests.[5] Equally challenged is the Republican National Committee, whose policies, candidates, and history offer nothing to the rising generation of voters.[6] There will be lessons to learn for the evangelical church from how these other social institutions navigate these same waters.

As a stopgap measure all older traditional evangelical pastors and institution leaders might consider hiring a nonbelieving millennial to serve as the resident "crap detector." (It is probable that this would become an honored millennial job title, "Resident Crap Detector.") In all seriousness, it is critical that steps be taken for "reverse mentoring." Here's how Alan Webber, the cofounder of *Fast Company* explains it: "It's a situation where the old fogies in an organization realize that by the time you're in your forties and fifties, you're not in touch with the future the same way the young twentysomethings are. They come with fresh eyes, open minds, and instant links to the technology of our future."[7] Reverse mentoring has been implemented in many of the leading companies in America. Most pastors will not be able to change our perspectives on reality fast enough to keep up with this millennial frame shift. It is best to have someone close by who can tell us how we are doing and coming across.

Millennials are both the hope of the church as well as being its most important challenge. It is imperative that church leaders grasp the coming contours of this cultural frame shift, which is most visibly seen in its millennial carriers. If there is lamenting to be done, it's over boomer church leaders' blindness to this shift and their reluctance to listen closely to their millennial peers. Listening will require more than tweaking one's college and young adult ministry; it will require reframing the posture of the entire church. This is surely a daunting task and not to be taken lightly. Nonetheless, like Captain Smith, you have been warned.

TAKEAWAYS FROM CHAPTER FIVE

- The evangelical church is losing the coming generation through a quiet drifting away, which will have serious long-term consequences to the church.
- The evangelical church is not the only social institution facing similar decline in millennial participation (i.e., the International Olympic Committee and the Republican National Party).

DISCUSSION QUESTIONS FOR CHAPTER FIVE

- How are millennials both the greatest hope and challenge to the evangelical church? How do we maximize the hope and minimize the challenge?
- How are millennials leaving the church? How much of this has already happened in your church?
- What might we learn from other social institutions who are struggling to reach millennials?

PART TWO

SIZING UP THE
IMPENDING FRAME SHIFT

One of the problems facing shipping in ice-infested waters is the inability of conventional marine radar to detect small floes of multiyear ice or dangerous glacial ice (such as bergy bits or growlers) early enough to avoid a collision.[1] Sometimes technology is not enough; we need to slow down and set a watch.

Similarly, the church must improve its detection of the contours and location of the coming frame shift. This section explores these questions: What are the contours of this coming frame shift? How does one get one's hands around it? What opportunities and challenges does it pose to the evangelical church?

SIX

THE VISIBLE SHIFT

From a distance one cannot really tell the power of an ocean wave. It is easier to judge when a surfer stands to attack the crest of the breaking wave. So, too, is the nature of this frame shift. When standing on the shore, watching the surfer will give us some visual perspective of the wave. Watching millennials is the best way to get some perspective on this coming frame shift. They didn't create the wave, but they are often the first ones up to ride it.

Culture by its very nature is an invisible force that greatly shapes our thoughts and behaviors. Because it is ubiquitous and invisible, some have wrongly assumed that it is unimportant.[1] In fact, it makes it doubly important, for if we ignore it, its power over us is compounded. To paraphrase University of Virginia sociologist James Davison Hunter, the power of culture is measured by the extent to which its definition of reality is realized in society and reinforced by those institutions that shape the social imaginary.[2] Philosopher Dallas Willard warns, "Ideas and images are the primary focus of Satan's efforts to defeat God's purposes with and for humankind. When we are subject to his chosen ideas and images, he can take a nap or a holiday."[3] If culture is water to a fish, the heat and toxicity of the water is everything to the fish, even if the fish is completely unaware of its environment.

There are aspects of this millennial culture shift that remain largely invisible. It may be all around us, but we don't notice it except to decry the inexplicable behavior of our millennial children. And this source of irritation is a key to recognizing their importance. Millennials are the first ones up on the wave, but they did not cause the wave or the rising tide. Millennials are the carriers of this shift in the social imaginary, but they did not cause it.

They represent the first post-Enlightenment and post-secular generational cohort. Not only are their perspectives different, they are better: a corrective to narrow, left-brained, overly certain analytical thinking that undermines the humble, holistic thinking that can embrace doubt and ambiguity. The New Copernican frame shift thesis is *not* based on cohort research, but, as we will discuss, on macrocultural trends of which millennials are the most visible carriers.

Social scientists readily acknowledge the difficulties in cohort research. For starters, you can't use science to determine the beginning and end points of one's sample set. This is why there is roughly a ten-year blurring of ages when describing millennials. For the purpose of this book I refer to millennials as those who reached adulthood around 2000. But there are no clear demarcations between Gen X and millennials, and millennials and Gen Z. Pop marketing articles aside, there is no respected science behind most of these proclamations.

As we discussed earlier, a cohort is an aggregate of individuals within a given population who experience the same event(s) within the same time interval. Cohort research assumes that a defined generation with common life experiences will give rise to distinctive values, attitudes, and behaviors.

Cohort research is most useful in medical epidemiology, when the variables of the sample can be controlled. When cohort research is applied to wider social descriptions, as is typical in marketing and business applications, too many variables come into play to be able to derive meaningful conclusions. It is difficult to disaggregate age, cohort, and period effects. A pair of marketing experts state the general academic opinion of this kind of research: "Cohort analysis involves inferring effects from observable differences. The causes of the effects can only be decided on the basis of evidence outside the cohort table."[4] The why to the observed effects cannot be determined from the analysis, because correlation is not causation.

The New Copernican thesis is not based on a cohort effect, which would limit it to shared life experiences of a defined demographic age grouping. Thus the potential audience for New Copernicans is greater than the 84 million millennials. It's a change in perspectives not merely based on a shared age group.

It is also important to note the difference between culture and politics. Culture is causally upstream from politics. It also involves longer-term trends. It is the difference between climate change and weather. The Trump presidency is weather and probably *not* reflective of the wider climate trends. Long-term the climate will be shaped more by the New Copernican ethos and less by Trump. In fact, the Trump presidency may very well accelerate this shift and its cultural implications.

It is also true that most millennials intuit the shift; they embody it but possess neither the language nor the categories to discuss it. They have a decidedly phenomenological and existential sensibility that is chronicled daily for all to see on their Facebook and Instagram posts. But they would have little appreciation for what this practice means about them. They don't have a language to describe their experience. Since the power of the culture is the power to define reality, this inability to articulate their sensibility and tendency to be silenced by the unwarranted criticism they receive is a weakness. Finding ways to give them a larger voice is one of the goals of this book.

However, before we completely discount the impact of millennial shared life experiences, just notice the significant list of culture-shaping events that took place during their formative years. Here is a partial list:

- Launch of the IBM personal desktop computer—1981
- California Task Force to Promote Self-Esteem and Personal Social Responsibility—1986
- The fragmenting of popular music—1980s
- The growing acceptance of hooking up—1990s
- Introduction of digital cable television—1990
- Launch of the Internet—1991
- Attack on the World Trade Center—2001
- Iraq War and the failure to find WMDs—2003
- Launch of Facebook—2004
- The first iPhone—2007
- Wall Street financial collapse—2007
- First black president—2008
- Black Lives Matter movement—2013
- NSA and WikiLeaks—2013
- Same-sex marriage legalized—2015

It does not take much imagination to see how in light of the collective impact of these culture-shaping technologies and events, the millennial generation would be highly connected, self-absorbed, cynical of institutional authority, and acutely aware of hyperpluralism.[5] Entire books have been written on the social and cultural impact of the rise of the self-esteem movement, the iPhone, 9/11, hookup culture, and same-sex marriage. Canadian philosopher and Templeton Prize winner Charles Taylor observes that in our search for individual authenticity, we cannot deny that our choices are made against a given cultural horizon. He writes, "It follows that one of the things we can't do, if we are to define ourselves significantly, is suppress or deny the horizons against which things take on significance for us."[6] Though different in content, these events and technologies are just as significant as the Great War and Depression were to millennials' grandparents.

The examination of millennials is enormously beneficial in getting at the contours and long-term significance of this New Copernican cultural frame. It becomes a highly efficient way of grasping this shift in the American social imaginary.[7] If forced to give reasons for this cultural shift, the cause of the wave that New Copernicans are riding, I would point to three factors: the experience of hyperpluralism, the rejection of the Enlightenment project, and the rejection of the secularization thesis.[8] We will examine the implications of each for the church over the course of the next three chapters.

TAKEAWAYS FROM CHAPTER SIX

- Culture is largely invisible, but enormously important.
- Millennials are not the causes of the frame shift, but as its carriers are the visible means by which one can come to understand the dynamics and contours of this frame shift in the social imaginary.

DISCUSSION QUESTIONS FOR CHAPTER SIX

- Why are most millennials unaware of the frame shift that they carry?
- Which of the culture-shaping events between 1980 and 2015 do you deem to be most influential in shaping this generation?
- How open are you to celebrating the unique characteristics of New Copernican millennials?

SEVEN

ALL WHO WANDER
ARE NOT LOST

Hitchhiking is one of the cheapest ways to travel. It is best to think of it as a walking adventure with the chance of getting a ride, more than anything else. People today are far more reluctant to pick up hitchhikers than in the past. One needs to be prepared to walk all day.

For most hitchhikers the adventure is the appeal, as much as a cheap mode of travel. There is an attitude of openness, an unscheduled chance encounter with a total stranger perhaps going in a similar direction. The journey is the point as much as the destination. The picture of a hitchhiker on an open road is an apt metaphor for New Copernicans.

Herein lies one of the largest and most important contrasts between New Copernicans and most evangelical leaders. It is the difference between being closed and open, dwellers and seekers. It represents a fundamental shift in attitude.

Father Tomáš Halík, Czech philosopher, priest, and 2014 Templeton Prize winner, has described this shift in the social imaginary as the shift from dwellers to seekers. Halík stated in the *New York Times,* "I think the crucial difference in the church today is not between so-called believers and nonbelievers, but between the dwellers and seekers." Dwellers are those who are happy where they are, who feel they have found the truth, while seekers, represented by New Copernicans, are those still looking for answers. Anyone can be an explorer: a Catholic, a Muslim, even an atheist. Halík believes that those in the community of seekers actually have more in common with one another than do seekers and dwellers from within the same faith tradition.[1]

A fundamentalist Christian and a fundamentalist atheist have more in common than a progressive Christian and a fundamentalist Christian.[2] The fundamentalists hold to their convictions with a closed fist, confident that they have a corner on the truth. On the other hand, the open Christian or atheist holds their convictions with an open hand, always willing to learn more and acutely aware that even at the points of their strongest convictions they might be wrong and that there is more to know than they currently comprehend. Billionaire investor and philanthropist Sir John Templeton called this "humility-in-theology."[3] In practice, dwelling and seeking is the difference between arrogance and humility.

It should not be taken as the difference between conviction and relativism. The shift is between those who have a closed and open mind-set, between those who have it all figured out and those who continue to learn. This shift makes a great deal of difference in tone, and is a defining cultural fault line. Dwellers, whether religious (fundamentalists), philosophical (foundationalists), or political (ideologues), are increasingly passé because this perspective is no longer on the front line and is receding from cultural relevance. It continues to exist in subcultural pockets, but is no longer cutting edge or broadly held.

Millennials are the poster children of seekers or explorers because they maintain an open mind and adopt a provisional attitude toward belief and reality, all the while longing for more. They embrace epistemological humility (the starting attitude), follow the scientific method and the explorer's quest (a process of open inquiry), and maintain a curious metaphysical openness to the laws of life wherever they may be found. They celebrate the journey, the exploration and the quest for new discoveries. They adopt the posture of a humble pilgrim or a courageous explorer rather than an arrogant teacher or know-it-all theologian.

These New Copernicans are aware that lived experience is not easily reduced to black-and-white categories. Lived reality is tainted with an uneasy and ever-changing mix of viewpoints and perspectives. The lines are blurred, the colors mixed, the motives conflicted. Reality is more 3-D than 2-D—more opaque angles than straightforward reasons, more picture than proposition, more poetry than prose.

This is not to say that truth does not exist, only that it does not come to us in a manner unmixed with doubt, confusion, and limitations. Pure truth is an abstraction, not a lived experience. Human knowledge is always mixed—a composite of truth and falsehood, belief and doubt, confidence and uncertainty. Human experience is intrinsically contingent, for our knowledge is always partial. Postmodernism has exposed the overly confident, unduly abstract nature of Enlightenment thinking.[4] It means that all that I believe I must accept with a measure of humility, an openness to correction, and a willingness to see the same truth from different angles—even or especially truth derived from reading the Bible.[5] James K. A. Smith concludes, "The picture of knowledge bequeathed to us by the Enlightenment is a forthright denial of our dependence, and it yields a Godlike picture of human reason."[6] In fact, we are not God nor do we have have Godlike knowledge.

Peter Enns's book *The Sin of Certainty* is a corrective to this kind of thinking, to a closed transcendent perspective—what Halík describes as dwellers. Enns argues that faith is a relational category best understood as trust, rather than a merely cognitive category associated with certainty.[7] The spiritual journey is best understood not as the results of a theological multiple-choice test, but as a relational adventure: more hitchhiking than a BarcaLounger, more open road than mental fortress. Historian Robert Wilken writes, "The first question, then, that a Christian intellectual should ask is not 'What should be believed?' or 'What should one think?' but '*Whom* should one trust?'"[8] Popular spiritual skeptic Michael McHargue adds "that the need for certainty is an addiction we can kick—that it's possible to have faith, and even follow Christ, without needing to defend historical Christianity like a doctoral thesis. We can approach beliefs not as gems to be mined from the earth and protected with clenched fists, but as butterflies that land on an open hand—as a gift to enjoy but not possess."[9] If faith is living, a closed fist will kill it.

At issue is not *what* I believe, but *how* many angles inform my faith. It is in this sense that we are all secular now. We are all touched by an acute awareness of alternative positions to our own. The price of pluralism and hypermodernity is an increased acceptance that all belief is contingent—infused from its inception with contestability, never held with absolute certainty. Truth exists, but it's not as clear or as easy to come to as some assume. Convictions are held with less binding address, with decreased plausibility, or influence on one's opinions. Such is the consequence of living in the midst of hyperpluralism.

Those who believe in absolute truth, or what Francis Schaeffer called "True Truth," find the admission to the limits of human knowledge hard to swallow. They hear relativism. But the polymath Michael Polanyi (who explores how tacit values influence scientific discovery) and most who have acknowledged a 3-D perspective after him do not embrace relativism.[10] Rather, they embrace humility, the possibility that some of our angles on the truth are incomplete and inadequate or just plain wrong. As the apostle Paul reminds us, "we know in part" (1 Cor. 13:9). It is actually good for our faith that we acknowledge this.

A consequence of the collapse of the Enlightenment project is a wider recognition of the 3-D nature of reality. With the insights of neuroscience, we've come to see that the assumed superiority of the left hemisphere of the brain has us seeing a 3-D landscape as a 2-D map. Much is lost in translation.

Neuroscience shows us that the West has long biased the brain's left hemisphere over the right and as a consequence has lost the ability to see reality as a whole. The evangelical church has followed along in this error. Philosophy has a tendency to be left-brained, but this has accelerated since the Enlightenment. The West has shifted to an either/or perspective on reality. This has been to our loss. McGilchrist explains,

In Western philosophy for much of the last 2,000 years, the nature of reality has been treated in terms of dichotomies. . . . Philosophy is naturally given, therefore, to a left-hemisphere version of the world, in which such divides as that between the subject and the object seem especially problematic. But these dichotomies may depend on a certain, naturally dichotomizing, "either/or" view of the world and may cease to be problematic in the world delivered by the right hemisphere, where what appears to the left hemisphere to be divided is unified, where concepts are not separated from experience, and where the grounding role of "betweenness" in constituting reality is apparent.[11]

In every conversation, listen for the frame: Is it either/or or both/and? As people who believe strongly in creation and the incarnation and the messiness it entails, Christians should naturally gravitate to 3-D lived experience over 2-D abstract fabrications. We would be wise to walk away from the Enlightenment's left-brained, either/or framing. This will require embracing ambiguity, paradox, and mystery, all of which are characteristics of Celtic spirituality and Eastern Orthodoxy. Left-brained thinking is the consequence of bad philosophy, reductionist theology, and erroneous neuroscience.

We would be wise to embrace complexity and contingency, humanness and fallibility. This is to adopt a humble attitude. As Sir John Templeton admonished, "Inherent in humility resides an open and receptive mind. We don't know all the answers to life, and sometimes not even the right questions have been revealed to us."[12] This is what is being advocated to us by New Copernicans, who are largely abandoning 2-D framing. For them it is a nonstarter. And from them we have much to learn. The Franciscan teacher-philosopher Richard Rohr warns, "Mature people are not either-or thinkers, but they bathe in the ocean of both-and. (Think Gandhi, Anne Frank, Martin Luther King Jr., Mother Teresa, Nelson Mandela, and the like.)"[13]

In moments of self-honesty, an appropriate fear arises from the admission that there might be additional angles I have not considered or mixed motives behind my rationalizations. That's the nature of 3-D spirituality. It's what the coming generation is looking for—an earthy, dirt-under-the-nails humanness. It should come as no surprise that New Copernicans prize lived experience, for hitchhiking is their natural mode of spiritual travel.

TAKEAWAYS FROM CHAPTER SEVEN

- The most important difference between evangelical leaders and New Copernicans is whether they are closed or open, dwellers or explorers.
- A closed perspective is held by those who feel that they have a corner on the truth and hold to their convictions with absolute certainty.
- An open perspective is held by those who hold their convictions with a provisional attitude, meaning they are aware that they have more to learn and that they could be wrong.
- This difference is not between conviction and relativism, but a difference in the attitude one takes toward truth and one's convictions.[14]
- New Copernicans are natural seekers and explorers.

DISCUSSION QUESTIONS FOR CHAPTER SEVEN

- Why is this shift from closed to open so threatening to evangelical leaders?
- How does this shift lay the groundwork for a change in attitude?
- Can one be open and still be willing to die for one's convictions?

EIGHT

EXPERIENCE
BEFORE THINKING

The French mathematician and Christian philosopher Blaise Pascal was a generation younger than René Descartes. The long shadow of Descartes's dictum, "I think, therefore I am," cast a rationalist pall over the emerging Enlightenment. If Descartes thought in algebraic terms, Pascal thought in geometric terms, left brain versus right brain. So it is not surprising that Pascal would state, "I can never forgive Descartes." For him reality cannot be fully captured by the rational mind: "We know truth, not only by the reason, but also by the heart."[1] Pascalian scholar Jean Laporte explains what Pascal had in mind: "If there is a legitimate place at all for the heart and its reasons, it is because reason does not exhaust either reality or the knowledge we have of reality. It is because reason is not enough for man, and perhaps not enough even for itself."[2] It is this rejection of a narrowing way of knowing that unites Pascal with New Copernicans. Former chancellor at Regent College James

Houston summarizes his contribution thus: "Pascal clearly saw that through reason alone one could not come to understand all of reality. Knowledge cannot ascertain the whole; it can only replace the wholeness with a pretension of the whole. In fact, the whole is replaced by reduction."[3] New Copernicans with Pascal affirm, "The heart has its reasons of which reason knows nothing; we know this in countless ways."[4] This is not an affirmation of subjectivism, but an awareness of the limits of reason and left-brain thinking. Philosopher Peter Kreeft expands, "Pascal does not oppose the heart to reason and demean reason by exalting the heart. On the contrary, he says the heart has its *reasons*. The heart does not only *feel,* it *sees*."[5] New Copernicans may not be versed in this history or philosophy, but this is how they process reality. They are a living critique of the Enlightenment project.

New Copernicans favor experiential learning. One of the most important characteristics of this shift is its bias against abstractions in favor of lived experience. Rather than have everything explained and laid out in theory, New Copernicans would rather muddle through experientially and figure it out on their own. They would rather live it through themselves than accept an abstract theoretical model or philosophical worldview first. The existential and the phenomenological take precedence over abstractions and theory (therefore rationalistic worldview instruction has limited value to them). They take their views from life, not authorities. Yes, this is a messy approach and inevitably filled with errors. But they are uniquely *their* errors.

Some may consider this a stubborn and even unfortunate trait, but it stems from their acute recognition that reality is more complex than can be easily put into words, propositions, and principles. You can't get at reality through left-brained abstractions. As we saw earlier, the left-brained approach leaves one in a "hall of mirrors."[6] New Copernicans prefer to start with the right hemisphere of the brain; they prefer experience, stories, and pictures—all that initially engages the imagination. They process reality from an engagement with the actual phenomena and not from hypothetical theories.

This means they prize the value of experience. This priority has educational and commercial implications. We talked earlier about how New Copernicans prefer to process reality from hand, heart, and then head: experience, imagination, and then analytic reason. This orientation will need to be taken into consideration in our schools, seminaries, and sermons. We need to reorient toward experiential learning away from abstractions.

But it also has commercial implications. Business consultant Joe Pine has written about the "experience economy."[7] He describes the fourfold progression of economic value from (1) extracting commodities, (2) to making goods, (3) to delivering services, and finally (4) to staging experiences.[8] He explains, "An experience occurs when a company intentionally uses services as the stage, and goods as props, to engage individual customers in a way that creates a memorable event."[9] Another way to measure this is whether what you are offering as an experience is a "selfie-worthy" moment. We now have composite words such as *shoppertainment*, *entertailing*, and *edutainment*, all of which build on this concept of commerce as entertainment. The underlying point is not fun and games or escapism, but the priority of lived experience, staging a participatory interactive drama. Pine explains that a key aspect of the experience is a connection, or an "environmental relationship, that unites the customer with the event or performance."[10] Pine lists four kinds of experiences: educational, escapist, esthetic, and entertainment.

Pine and Gilmore followed up Pine's first book on the experience economy with *Authenticity: What Consumers Really Want.*[11] Authenticity is the desire for something that feels real. There is a performative or dramatic aspect to experience—for New Copernicans, all of life is a staged event—and with it the desire to be given a central role within the staged drama.[12] Consequently, mobile phones at the ready means any event can become the next YouTube reality featurette. Life is a staged drama waiting to happen, finally validated and authenticated by the video. As is commonly stated, "Pics or it didn't happen."

Recently I was in New York City when a Hispanic skateboarder almost hit a black man crossing in the pedestrian walkway. Curses were expressed loudly. Mothers were implicated. The skateboarder stopped and came back to face the now enraged black man. Instantly a dramatic altercation unfolded. Four characters stepped forward to center stage in the middle of this New York City street: the insulted skater, the angry pedestrian, a Good Samaritan passerby who sought to keep the two men from coming to blows, and the cell-phone videographer. The videographer was not trying to do anything to influence the burgeoning fight. He was simply there to record what was happening and might happen. He was there to validate the experience. There is evidently a very thin line between life and reality TV. The drama of life is in many cases a videoworthy subject as is demonstrated by numerous television shows built on this premise. These are illustrations of the priority New Copernicans place on lived experience over book knowledge or abstractions.

Consumer research shows that 78 percent of millennials prefer experiences to things. This is driving the rent-to-buy phenomenon and the sharing economy. In 2015, 51 percent of millennials had used a sharing economy service such as Uber, Airbnb, Rent the Runway, and Zipcar. Weddings in this context are less about the marriage ceremony and more about "creating memories that last a lifetime" for the guests. This is a generation that prioritizes human connection and new experiences.[13]

On a tranquil night Matthew McConaughey walks to the pool in his designer dress suit for an impromptu dive into the pool— it's unexpected, impetuous, refreshing, and exhilarating. We cut to him driving his 2017 Lincoln MK7 with the caption, "It's like that." Here Lincoln is not selling a car, but the feeling of an experience associated with it.[14]

According to an Eventbrite study, eight in ten millennials said experiences help shape their identity and create lifelong experiences.[15] Running has had a renewed surge in popularity not because of traditional 10K events or marathons, but because of nontraditional extreme events such as Tough Mudder, the Color Run, and the Spartan Race. According to *Running USA*, in 2013 more runners participated in nontraditional races than traditional events, such as half-marathons and marathons, a fortyfold growth since 2009.[16] The goal of these events is finishing, having fun, and doing it with friends: unique memorable events that are selfie-worthy. MOB-sters (mud-obstacles-beer), as mudder participants are called, often wear costumes, are chased by zombies, or run through color or foam. This is a very different athletic experience than the straitlaced traditional running events where competition, individual achievement, and winning are paramount. This is sport stemming from a different ethos. This is New Copernican athletics.

From this perspective we have much to learn and appreciate. The New Copernican sensibility is highly incarnational. It is bawdy, relational, tactile, and experiential. It is not clean, clear, and cognitive. Along the same lines, New Copernican spirituality is messy and embodied. It has parallels with ancient Celtic spirituality—that form of Christian practice that emerged in Britain and Ireland in the fourth and fifth centuries under the leadership of Saint Patrick and Saint Brigid.[17] Like Celtic spirituality, New Copernican spirituality has dirt under its nails and is suffused with the smells and messiness of life. We'd best take our cues from Jesus, who was born in an animal barn and placed in a manger filled with straw and died on a wooden cross with nails through his hands and feet. We'd do well not to lose the smell of the barn or the splinters of the cross. Much of modern-day evangelicalism has lost this embodied incarnational feel in favor of a sanitized, cognitive, Gnostic head trip.[18] To do so is to lose the reality and scope of Christ's work.

So the millennial carriers of the New Copernican shift represent an explorer's attitude and experiential orientation; the frame shift's post-Enlightenment character is seen in their openhandedness and humility in truth-seeking and their affirmation of lived experience over abstract theory. Finally, the frame shift's post-secular nature is revealed in New Copernicans' haunted openness to the transcendent. We turn now to grasping what post-secular means.

TAKEAWAYS FROM CHAPTER EIGHT

- New Copernicans favor experiential learning; the existential and the phenomenological take precedence over abstractions and theory.
- Learning happens best through experience, imagination, and then analytical reason: hand, heart, head—not head, heart, hand.

- An experience happens when one uses service as the stage and the goods as the props to engage individuals in a way that creates a memorable event.
- Authenticity is the desire for something that is felt to be real.
- Seventy-eight percent of millennials prefer experiences to things. Eighty percent said experiences help shape their identity.
- New Copernican spirituality, like Celtic spirituality, is messy and embodied; it has dirt under its fingernails.

DISCUSSION QUESTIONS FOR CHAPTER EIGHT

- How is this experiential bias a natural extension from New Copernicans' post-Enlightenment bias?
- Do you feel that your church experience is about gaining information versus building a spiritual relationship?
- What are some of the most memorable spiritual experiences that you have had? What made them so?
- How would embracing this preference for experience and the experiential change the way we preach or teach discipleship?

NINE

CRACKS IN THE WALL

In a darkened room it doesn't take a large crack to let in some light. Even the smallest fissure letting in a glimmer of light is like a lighthouse beacon; it portends another world, to something more than the darkness. The smallest glimmer can be a luminous beacon of hope.

There are today four basic orientations to reality, what we have described as social imaginaries: closed transcendent, closed immanent, open immanent, and open transcendent (see figure on the next page).[1] The dividing line down the middle of these four alternatives represents the fundamental frame shift we have been discussing. The left side represents dwellers, those adopting the illusionary certainty of the Enlightenment. The right represents those who hold an open, exploring posture toward reality. About dwellers, neuroscientist Iain McGilchrist observes, "In the field of religion there are dogmatists of no-faith as there are of faith, and both seem to me closer to one another than those who try to keep open the door to the possibility of something beyond the customary ways in which we think, but which we would have to find, painstakingly, for our-selves."[2] There are religious and atheistic fundamentalists—both have a closed take on reality.

FOUR SOCIAL IMAGINARIES
Lens of the "Good Life"

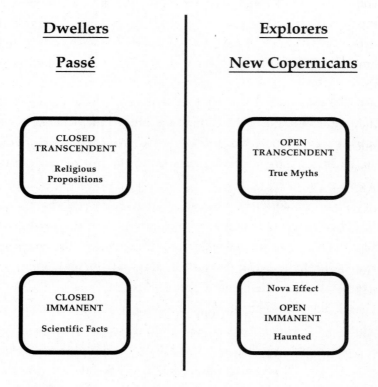

Dwellers | **Explorers**

Passé | New Copernicans

CLOSED TRANSCENDENT

Religious Propositions

OPEN TRANSCENDENT

True Myths

CLOSED IMMANENT

Scientific Facts

Nova Effect

OPEN IMMANENT

Haunted

We have argued that the closed transcendents (typified by church-based evangelicals) and closed immanents (typified by university-based New Atheists) are increasingly culturally passé.[3]

They represent existing tribes, which, though they still have a large following, are no longer dominant or influential among those who curate the contemporary cultural social imaginary. It is my belief that closed transcendents and closed immanents—and those institutions that they represent—will be subject to growing cultural irrelevance. Their days of cultural influence are numbered.

This should be a wake-up call to closed transcendent evangelical institutions—particularly churches, seminaries, and Christian colleges and universities. New Atheist writers are already shifting their dogmatic rhetoric to appeal more to open immanent explorers.[4] They clearly see the handwriting on the wall. While I am not predicting the end of evangelicalism, I am suggesting that the cultural trends suggest an inevitable weakening of the closed transcendent perspective. It will not disappear, but will slowly dwindle and become decreasingly relevant on the cultural front lines. This is already being seen in seminary enrollment. Soon closed transcendent evangelicalism will exist only as a quaint Amish curiosity. Peter Berger warns, "The world-building potency of religion is restricted to the construction of sub-worlds, of fragmented universes of meaning, the plausibility of which may in some cases be no larger than the nuclear family."[5] This is not a future that God desires. There is, however, a silver lining to this story for those willing to listen.

There is an incredible opportunity for the church. The arena where there is the greatest potential for spiritual cultural influence is among open immanents—the very social imaginary where most young people and New Copernicans are found.

Unlike the New Atheists, who subscribe to metaphysical naturalism or what sociologist Peter Berger calls "a world without windows," New Copernicans affirm the crack in the wall, the glimmer of light from beyond.[6] New Copernicans assume a secular frame, the absence of God or gods, *but* have at the same time a nagging sense of incompleteness. Though they are generally naturalist in orientation in contrast to supernaturalists, New Copernicans are not closed naturalists (as is typical of New Atheists) and are thus open to the possibility of transcendence, to an "inter-cosmic mystery."[7] They are haunted by the possibility of something more.

One hears this in the opening sentence of Julian Barnes's novel, *Nothing to Be Frightened Of,* "I do not believe in God, but I miss him."[8] You see it in Frank Schaeffer's *Why I Am an Atheist Who Believes in God*.[9] From a closed transcendent perspective, this title makes no sense. It is however perfectly New Copernican.

One hears this haunted longing in bestselling author Elizabeth Gilbert's comments: "I've spent my entire life in devotion to creativity, and along the way I've developed a set of beliefs about how it works—and how to work with it—that is unapologetically based upon magical thinking. And when I refer to magic here, I mean it literally. Like, in the Hogwarts sense. I am referring to the supernatural, the mystical, the inexplicable, the surreal, the divine, the transcendent, the otherworldly."[10]

These composite longings are expressed each summer at the Burning Man Festival, the aspirational cultural zeitgeist event where neo-pagan spirituality and sexuality mix with performance art and social justice utopianism.[11] This is what we mean by New Copernicans being post-secular. This openness to mystery creates a cultural condition that philosopher Charles Taylor describes as the "Nova Effect," an explosion of different options for belief and meaning—from vampire and zombie movies to bells-and-smells high-church rituals. Like C. S. Lewis before his conversion, they travel comfortably in the mythic world of Neil Gaiman's *American*

Gods. What one finds is a proliferation of spiritual options and alternative spiritual expressions as are commonly discussed on *The Moth Radio Hour* or *On Being.*

To be candid, the Nova Effect is a spiritual reality around which most evangelicals feel very uncomfortable. It is hard for them to withhold their judgmental assessment toward quasi-paganism or New Age pap. It is hard for them to see past the nudity at Burning Man to the spiritual hauntedness that permeates the festival. Few can conceive of this as a valued on-ramp for spiritual connection.

With this as background, one can better understand the erroneous way this spiritual expression is described as the "rise of religious nones," a descriptor that New Copernicans totally reject. This is not the growth of atheism but the rise of DIY spirituality.[12]

This is not a totally new spiritual trajectory. We do well to remember the spiritual journey of C. S. Lewis, who moved from a closed transcendent perspective in his youthful Belfast Anglicanism to closed immanent atheism in his teen years, to an open immanent viewpoint under the influence of Yeats and Norse myths while in graduate school, and then to an open transcendent conclusion through the guidance of J. R. R. Tolkien and Hugo Dyson.[13] Many today are retracing Lewis's steps. Michael McHargue, aka "Science Mike," tells a similar story in his book, *Finding God in the Waves: How I Lost My Faith and Found It Again Through Science.*[14] Sorely missing today are people like Tolkien and Dyson, people who understand an apologetics of the imagination, are comfortable in the world of myth, and can move people from Joseph Campbell to Jesus Christ, from universal myths to "myths that really happened."

New Copernicans live in an open immanent social imaginary. In order to reach them the church must learn to build on their sense of haunting, their ongoing suspicion that there is more to life than meets the eye. The church must also learn to adopt New Copernicans' relational, experience-driven approach to learning, and respect their muddling-through-with-friends approach to life.

Little is being done currently to equip pastors for this task. Instead, most of the religious debates and public engagements with culture, sponsored by groups such as Veritas Forums, are confrontations between closed transcendents and closed immanents, between religious evangelicals and academic atheists, which—as far as culture is concerned—are largely beside the point. For New Copernicans they engender a yawn.

Evangelical pastor Tim Keller had the opportunity to discuss faith and spiritual seeking with *New York Times* columnist Nicholas Kristof in the piece "Am I a Christian, Pastor Timothy Keller?"[15] While it is highly notable that a thoughtful evangelical voice was given such prominence in the *New York Times* and while acknowledging that it may have been impossible to reframe the interview, it was largely a missed opportunity. As a closed immanent (presumably a New Atheist member of the media), Kristof established the frame for the interview, which was more about cognitive boundary maintenance of his own biases than open pilgrimaging and genuine seeking.

"Does one have to believe in the resurrection of Jesus or the virgin birth to be a Christian?" Kristof asked. Keller took the bait. What if Keller had countered with "Nicholas, these are interesting questions, but the wrong starting question for a person like you"? What would have been interesting would have been a discussion about what it would take to move Kristof from a closed immanent perspective to an open immanent one. What if a relationship with Jesus is more like falling in love than answering the questions on a philosophy or history exam? Here a left-brained question was answered with a left-brained answer—when what was needed most was the challenge of a right-brained counter-question. Kristof needs more poetry, not more propositions. What we got was an intellectual impasse, rather than the beginning of a humble exploration of a relational experience.

Those who have rejected the closed transcendent perspective of American evangelicalism are generally made to feel unwelcome and have subsequently left the church. "Oh, he's a liberal," becomes the quick, immediate dismissal. One thinks of Rachel Held Evans, Peter Enns, and Frank Schaeffer, to name three.[16] We may not always agree with where they have landed in terms of lifestyle or theology; however, we must learn to accept and appreciate their sensitivity to the emerging New Copernican frame and respect their fight to find authentic expressions of faith within it. They are the prophets of the New Copernican sensibility.

The life trajectories represented by Evans and Schaeffer are instructive. Their journeys are messy and painful. They can hardly talk about their spiritual journeys and their encounters with the church without anger. While I'm sure that there is fault on both sides, closed transcendent institutions have a tendency to emotionally brutalize high-profile detractors. Consequently, these prophetic voices' forward-looking progressive insights are often laced with understandable bitterness and various degrees of anger toward the evangelical institutions from which they are now distant or rejected. There is a growing number following in their footsteps, people who describe themselves as "spiritually frustrated and homeless."[17] The evangelical church needs to find a way to provide genuine seekers like this—with all their unorthodoxy, doubt, and confusion—a home and a safe place to ask unsafe questions.

However, even now there are few opportunities provided

within the church to allow people—especially children of closed transcendent parents or students at closed transcendent colleges and universities—the space to grow into a more thoughtful and humane faith expression. Instead, we push these people unintentionally toward atheism—by forced silenced and assumed shaming. As we discussed earlier, church experience is fostering skepticism among the young.[18] At the very least we could stop pushing people away and embrace this muddled longing as an on-ramp for fruitful spiritual seeking. Perhaps we could even learn something from them in the process, like the courage and vulnerability to express our own confusion aloud.

New Copernicans are the carriers of a new social imaginary that is post-Enlightenment and post-secular. Theirs is an experiential, open exploration of a haunted world. These are the hitchhikers we pass by each day. We need to join *their* pilgrimage.

TAKEAWAYS FROM CHAPTER NINE

- There are four basic orientations to reality or social imaginaries: closed transcendent, closed immanent, open immanent, and open transcendent.
- Closed transcendent and closed immanent are increasingly culturally passé.
- Closed transcendent evangelicalism will exist only as a quaint Amish curiosity.
- New Copernicans affirm a "world with windows," a reality that is open to and penetrated by the transcendent, a magical haunted world.
- The Nova Effect is the explosion of different options for

belief and meaning in such an open transcendent world—from Tibetan Buddhism to Deep Ecology to New Age mysticism.

- The rise of religious nones is not a rise in atheism but a rise in DIY spirituality.
- We lack people who can encourage seekers to move from an open immanent to an open transcendent perspective.

DISCUSSION QUESTIONS FOR CHAPTER NINE

- How does this openness to a magical world change our approach to apologetics?
- How does the Nova Effect create an opportunity and a challenge to the evangelical church?
- Are you walking in pilgrimage with one of these eclectic New Copernican spiritual seekers? What have you learned from them?

PART THREE

RESPONSES TO
THE WARNING

This pan-pan warning about the New Copernican shift in the social imaginary is both a challenge and opportunity for the church. Of the four current social imaginaries operating today in American society, two are culturally passé and two are pregnant with opportunity. Over the course of the next four chapters we will look at each more closely. Our assessing the situation, determining where we are in our own spiritual journey, and prioritizing our efforts will make all the difference.

TEN

SELF-RIGHTEOUS BLINDNESS

The first of the social imaginaries we will explore is the closed transcendent perspective. This represents the group with which many readers of this book will be most familiar and be most prone to defend. There is an inherent confidence and brittleness to a closed transcendent perspective.

The picture we should keep in mind is General George Armstrong Custer. Custer was a West Point graduate in the class of 1862. He graduated at the bottom of his class. He was a bit of a renegade, the kind of person who didn't think the rules applied to him. He was almost expelled each year at West Point, graduating with one of the worst conduct records in the history of the academy. And yet he was a natural leader who achieved a distinguished record in the Civil War, eventually commanding the Michigan Cavalry Brigade. He was promoted to general at the age of twenty-three, one of the youngest generals in the war. He fought courageously in many major Civil War battles. One of his men killed Confederate cavalry officer General J. E. B. Stuart at Yellow Tavern, but Custer became famous for leading the campaign that led to Lee's surrender at Appomattox.

But none of that is what Custer is remembered for in history. He is remembered for his rash attack at Little Big Horn that led to the total annihilation of his cavalry division, called in popular history Custer's Last Stand. Hubris sank the *Titanic* and defeated Custer's cavalry. It need not also defeat the church. Evangelical leaders cannot count on past success as they now face the growing implications of this New Copernican frame shift. History will not judge them kindly if they do not pay attention to this new missional opportunity.

Those who find themselves in the closed transcendent social imaginary have an unquestioned certainty about their position, which is held without much self-awareness. They are in the "telling business" because they are right and others are wrong. Life for them is black-and-white. Their truth is an either/or category. Reality is a binary universe filled with right and wrong. Faith is primarily a cognitive category about beliefs, and enormous energy is expended clarifying and maintaining cognitive belief boundaries—inerrancy, evolution, and traditional marriage are some recent battles that come to mind. This is a view totally reinforced by left-hemisphere Enlightenment thinking.

There are at least three major intellectual problems with this view, which we have discussed earlier. First, this confidence is based on a faulty view of human knowledge and an erroneous view of faith. This is then reinforced by distorted neuroscience. One of the great benefits of postmodernism has been its challenge to the hubristic assumptions of modernist epistemology.[1] The composite of these views is intellectual arrogance coupled with an inherent judgmentalism.

These views breed a Pharisaical attitude, which Jesus specifically warns us against. "To some who were confident of their own righteousness and looked down on everyone else, Jesus told this parable" (Luke 18:9). Generally, when the Luke 18:9–14 passage is preached, it is used to refer to moral superiority or self-righteousness, not intellectual rightness. But they go hand in hand. The attitudes they foster are corrosive to both faith and witness. Jesus warns us, "For all those who exalt themselves will be humbled, and those who humble themselves will be exalted" (Luke 18:14).

Intellectually, we would do well to return to an ancient faith expressed prior to the Enlightenment. Philosopher James K. A. Smith writes, "I will argue that the postmodern church could do nothing better than be ancient, that the most powerful way to reach a postmodern world is by recovering tradition."[2] Genuine people of faith embracing the New Copernican ethos must "refuse to be haunted by Cartesian anxiety."[3] This means rejecting modernity's quasi-omniscient certainty. Smith concludes, "Those whose Christian experience has been shaped by American fundamentalism are particularly open and receptive to this critique of determinate modern religion since we have seen and experienced firsthand the kind of harm that is done—both to people and the gospel—by such practices and theological formulations."[4] Our position here is that we must reject both the modernist's objectivism and the postmodernist's skepticism. Smith points his readers to Augustine and Aquinas.[5] I tend to find great resonance with Celtic spirituality.[6] In short, we will need to learn to be post-Enlightenment. One way to do this is to align with pre-Enlightenment spirituality.

But the intellectual difficulties of this shift are further compounded by the existential damage done by the tone this modernist posture takes. One rarely gets to the epistemological debates with

New Copernicans because they are already turned off by the tone we take in our public affirmations of faith. They do not hear contingency or humility, and thus the entirety of our faith is written off as inauthentic.

Again, I am not advocating for the absence of convictions or the embrace of either skepticism or relativism, only the self-awareness that my knowledge is limited and my proclivity for error is real. We need to hold our convictions and beliefs with an open hand suffused with humility. We must move from closed to open, from dweller to explorer. The most important difference between people is between those for whom life is a quest and those for whom it is not. As long as we portray the sense that we have a corner on truth and that we have nothing to learn from others, the conversation with New Copernicans will remain closed.

We have a powerful exemplar of the difference this makes in Pope Francis. He has not changed Catholic doctrine, but he has single-handedly changed the tone in which the doctrine is heard and encountered. Closed transcendent Catholics rail against him. Meanwhile he appears on the cover of *Rolling Stone* magazine. This pope understands the dynamics of the New Copernican frame shift. He states, "The Christian who 'wants everything clear and safe . . . will find nothing.' Tradition and memory of the past must help us to have the courage to open up new areas to God. The church was wrong in the past in accepting slavery and the death penalty. 'Ecclesiastical rules and precepts that were once effective . . . have now lost value or meaning.' The church must 'grow in its understanding' and 'mature in its judgment.'"[7] Here is a pope who places pastoral care before doctrinal boundary maintenance. "Who am I to judge?" he responded when asked about homosexuality. Instead he encourages homosexual seekers to pursue a love relationship with God. He is not willing to let the church be known for side issues when the joy of love is primary.[8] He is a person in whom modern New Copernicans can see Christ. Evangelical Jim Daly has done much the same at Focus on the Family in his efforts to soften the image of the organization as seen in his public friendship with prominent LGBT activist Ted Trimpa. The *New York Times* reporter writes, "Mr. Daly continued what has been the signal initiative of his term at the evangelical group: transforming an organization associated with the divisive strife of the culture wars into one that invites civil dialogue with its religious and ideological foes."[9]

We need to do a much better job of matching our music to our lyrics, to allow the beauty of the gospel to be evident in how we talk to others, how we see ourselves, and how we present our convictions. Catholic spokesman of Pope John Paul II's Theology of the Body Christopher West reminds us that "the Christian message is often set to the wrong music, or it is not set to music at all. When this happens, Christianity becomes dry, cold, and seemingly irrelevant to the real desires of the heart."[10] Can we win the question with beauty and music? Can we speak first to the imagination and heart? Isn't this the lesson of the compelling film *Babette's Feast*?[11]

Moving beyond a closed transcendent perspective may be more human, more beautiful, more winsome, but we must acknowledge that for the evangelical pastor it is fraught with danger. Many a ministry career has been lost on these judgmental shoals. Any transition away from this closed transcendent social imaginary must proceed with wisdom. It is best to navigate with a chart to understand the alternative social imaginaries and to affirm the reality of the frame shift. My concern here is not simply with youth ministry or reaching college students and young adults, but rather with acknowledging the implications of this shift for the future validity of one's entire ministry.

Theologian Megan DeFranza highlights the question pointedly at pastors in her essay "Disappearing Our Pastors." She writes, "Our churches, denominations, and schools send us off to get our PhDs but then expect us to come back and teach the same things they have always known. They don't *really* want us to learn; instead they want our credentials to shore up the homestead. . . . Can we create space in our churches and educational institutions for pastors and leaders to continue their journeys without driving them to the lonesome desert, the suffocating closet, or the grave?"[12] She quotes from Wendell Berry's novel *Jayber Crow*, "How can I preach if I don't have any answers?" What we see is that it is not possible unless one is willing to make the frame shift. Then we can get off our theological soapbox and enter into the kindred pilgrimage called life.

Without this shift in tone and emphasis, this openness to exploration, meaningful conversations with New Copernicans will be greatly thwarted. Is it possible to preach from questions rather than from answers? What makes Pope Francis a revolutionary is that he has adopted a new frame. We can join him in this frame.

Is there really a choice in the matter? The frame shift is happening. The reality will not go away. Custer was a flamboyant, charismatic leader, not unlike many megachurch pastors. His courage has been rarely questioned. The combination of arrogance and poor reconnaissance was his undoing. History need not repeat itself.

TAKEAWAYS FROM CHAPTER TEN

- Those who hold a closed transcendent social imaginary have an unquestioned certainty about their position, which is held without much self-awareness.

- The closed transcendent social imaginary operates with an either/or mind-set.
- An open perspective means that one is aware that one's knowledge is limited and one's proclivity for error real. Convictions are held with an open hand suffused with humility.
- Pope Francis is an exemplar of an open transcendent perspective.
- We need to match our music to our lyrics, our tone and attitude to the beauty of the gospel.

DISCUSSION QUESTIONS FOR CHAPTER TEN

- In what way is George Custer like evangelical church leaders today?
- What are the three intellectual problems with a closed transcendent mind-set?
- Have you had an experience or conversion that pushed you toward an open transcendent perspective? What was it like?
- Where does the music need to better match the lyrics in your life?

ELEVEN

RELIGIOUSLY TONE-DEAF

The rise of militant evangelistic atheism has been met with some alarm. Repeated best sellers are being released by a team of intellectuals who have been called the "Four Horsemen of the Non-Apocalypse": Richard Dawkins (*The God Delusion*), Christopher Hitchens (*God Is Not Great*), Sam Harris (*The End of Faith*), and Daniel Dennett (*Breaking the Spell*).[1] According to Dawkins, "We are all atheists about most of the gods that societies have ever believed in. Some of us just go one god further."[2]

Paralleling the public recognition of New Atheism has been the growth of religious nones, that segment of the population that has no identifiable religious affiliation. This growth is particularly large among young people. But as we have seen, these two categories— New Atheists and religious nones—should not be conflated as they represent two distinct social imaginaries.

New Atheists are the secular equivalent of religious funda-mentalists. They are most likely to be found within the academy with some crossover in media and entertainment. Their approach toward truth has the same kind of objectivist absolutism as religious fundamentalists, as they have the same reliance on left-hemisphere Enlightenment rationalism.

It is not surprising then to see numerous debates between these opposing viewpoints. Much of apologetic instruction within the evangelical church is aimed at discrediting their assertions. The topics of evolution and Marxism are often central in these debates.

I was recently speaking to a group of young people in New York City who are active in Black Lives Matter. On this particular night there were older women attending who were members of the Revolutionary Communist Party, a Maoist organization. They were friends with the young people and protest cobelligerents in their shared outrage against police brutality. These older women forcefully presented their orthodox Marxist doctrine, the likes of which I had not heard since graduate school. The women were getting nowhere with these young activists.

"We believe that the revolution can happen differently, without violence," one young activist said.

Frustrated, one of the communist women blurted, "Do you believe in God?"

"Yes," the New Copernican activist replied.

"Well, we're atheists," the older woman responded confidently. The young people literally rolled their eyes. I listened with amazement. Though the content was different, the atheists' argument was framed in just the same manner as a Christian fundamentalist might address his or her followers. It was clear to me that in spite of their friendship and shared life experience, the two groups were talking right past each other in exactly the same manner that typifies the church's experience with millennials. Closed immanents were talking to open immanents in a manner that made no sense to them. The communication obstacles they were facing were exactly the same as those facing religious closed transcendents.

It is true that militant atheists have found their voice within American society. One thinks of the popularity of comedian Bill Maher and the HBO political talk show *Real Time with Bill Maher*. Maher has disdain, disgust, and derision for all religions and religious believers. Religious believers are, in his mind, intellectually stupid and opposed to science. To him the average American is stupid. While it is true that Maher is an intellectual elitist and religiously tone-deaf, religious believers must be honest enough to acknowledge that he has a point. There is a strong anti-intellectual, antiscience bias in American evangelicalism. Evangelical historian Mark Noll was honest enough to state, "The scandal of the evangelical mind is that there is not much of an evangelical mind."[3]

This scandal is not lost on New Copernicans, who are themselves disgusted with the antiscience posture of evangelicals when it comes to matters such as climate change. Evangelical leaders would serve themselves well watching *Real Time with Bill Maher* or his 2008 film, *Religulous*, to appreciate how we are perceived by cultural elites.

It is important to make this appreciative point about closed immanent intellectuals and New Atheism before also acknowledging that their views are increasingly passé. Obviously there are some internal problems with their arguments; Dawkins and Hitchens in particular are prone to rash statements and hyperbole. But this is not their major problem. One has to determine whether the cultural glow of the New Atheists is the dawn of something new or the sunset of something that is passing. The closed immanent perspective is increasingly out of touch with the cultural front line. It is a binary either/or rationalist fundamentalism that is no longer in sync with the cultural zeitgeist. Historian Reza Aslan writes in the *Washington Post*:

> There is, as has often been noted, something peculiarly evangelistic about what has been termed the new atheist movement. . . .
> It is no exaggeration to describe the movement . . . as a new and particularly zealous form of fundamentalism—an atheist fundamentalism. The parallels with religious fundamentalism are obvious and startling: the conviction that they are in the sole possession of truth, the troubling lack of tolerance for the views of their critics, the insistence on a literalist reading of scripture, the simplistic reductionism of the religious phenomenon, and their overwhelming sense of siege.[4]

This perspective is just as alien to New Copernicans as religious evangelicals.[5]

Nor is this simply a problem for philosophy or religion. On the science front, genetics, cosmology, astrophysics, and neuroscience are all pointing to a world that is compatible with belief in transcendence.[6] Neuroscience is being used to question the very foundations of rational thought and the limits of science.[7] Medical neurologist Robert Burton writes, "My goal is to strip away the power of certainty by exposing its involuntary neurological roots. If science can shame us into questioning the nature of conviction, we might develop some degree of tolerance and increased willingness to consider alternative ideas."[8] It is not surprising that Mike McHargue was able to make sense of his mystical religious experience through the study of neuroscience.[9]

The humility called for by the New Copernican shift cuts as deeply into science as it does theology. It touches both forms of fundamentalism. An increasing number of atheists are coming to appreciate this and are distancing themselves from antireligious vitriol and the closed immanent perspective. Chris Stedman is a leader in this effort. He writes, "I believe that broadening the aims of the atheist movement to be more affirming and less antagonistic will mean that it will have more to offer people—that it will contribute something positive to their lives."[10] An open atheism is also seen in New York University philosophy professor Thomas Nagel, who, as an atheist, questions the status quo assumptions about a "world without windows."[11] He writes, "My skepticism is not based on religious belief, or on a belief in any definite alternative. It is just a belief that the available scientific evidence, in spite of the consensus of scientific opinion, does not in this matter rationally require us to subordinate the incredulity of common sense."[12] Many young people are consequently coming back to a view espoused by Albert Einstein, "Science without religion is lame; religion without science is blind."[13] Sadly, there are not many safe places within the church to discuss or hold these views. What are apparent contradictions to some are perfectly acceptable to a New Copernican, which is why few are attracted to or remain long within the closed immanent social imaginary. If they stay, it is mostly out of anger to the church of their youth—more of an angry reaction than a settled choice. The settled young nonbeliever untainted by the church has a very different profile. We turn, then, to examine the social imaginary where most New Copernicans are found, the open immanent frame.

TAKEAWAYS FROM CHAPTER ELEVEN

- New Atheism is not where we should be focusing our attention.
- New Atheists are the equivalent of religious fundamentalists.

- New Copernicans are disgusted with the antiscience posture of evangelicals.
- There is a growing compatibility within scientific disciplines and the belief in transcendence.

DISCUSSION QUESTIONS FOR CHAPTER ELEVEN

- In what ways is New Atheism culturally passé?
- How does scientism mirror religious fundamentalism?
- Where do we see openness to transcendence in science?

TWELVE

HAUNTED DOUBTERS

New Copernicans come in a wide variety of personalities and types. German sociologist Max Weber developed the conceptual tool of the *ideal type*. He recognized that no scientific system is ever capable of reproducing the complexity of reality. One has to generalize and in some sense develop an abstraction. "An ideal type is a concept constructed by a social scientist to capture the principal features of some social phenomena."[1] The key to developing an ideal type is to immerse oneself in historical reality and derive the types from that analysis. At their best, an ideal type should be neither too specific nor too general. Ideal types are a heuristic device, a teaching tool to examine a slice of historical reality.

New Copernicans are an ideal type. While most people hate being labeled, millennials are particularly sensitive to this, as they consistently feel like they have been mislabeled. I have received a lot less pushback on the New Copernican label from millennials, but I am aware that its features are not uniformly the same. Christian millennials are generally the most varied from the ideal type of

New Copernican, as they tend to mix a lot of the old paradigm in with the new. They are hybrid New Copernicans. Christian millennials tend to have a lot of cognitive dissonance, having one foot in and one foot out. They are the paradigm straddlers. Some pastors have suggested that our current outreach to millennials is largely with hybrid New Copernicans and not genuine New Copernicans. They anticipate that the task of reaching genuine New Copernicans will become more difficult.

To get at the ideal type of New Copernicans you have to look at the Burning Man Festival in Black Rock City, Nevada. Your awareness of Burning Man and your attitude toward the festival is a pretty good indicator of whether you are a dweller or explorer. The Burning Man Festival will not be everyone's cup of tea, but its edgy outrageousness makes it a useful foil in discussing New Copernicans.

For the uninitiated, Burning Man is a countercultural festival held each year in the desert north of Reno, Nevada, during the last week of August. It attracts 50,000 to 70,000 people each year to Black Rock Desert, a temporary metropolis that is dedicated to community, art, self-expression, and self-reliance. It is a combination of a nudist camp, Occupy Wall Street, Green Peace, and Cirque du Soleil. There is no water, electricity, Internet, or any of the modern conveniences there—just fine dust, high heat, and extreme cold. To navigate 70,000 people under these harsh conditions for a week is a marvel of planning and self-reliance. A bedrock premise of the festival is to "leave no trace." Great lengths are taken to return the desert back to its pristine untouched condition after each festival. Another marvel.

More than a festival, Burning Man is a movement, now with smaller festivals held around the world. It began in 1986 on a local beach in San Francisco, produced by founder Larry Harvey. The event takes its name from the symbolic ritual burning of a large wooden effigy ("the Man") that traditionally occurs on the Saturday evening of the event. Today it stands as the Super Bowl of contemporary countercultural expression, attracting Hollywood A-listers and Silicon Valley executives. Tesla and SpaceX's CEO Elon Musk famously said, "Burning Man is Silicon Valley."[2] Burning Man has become a living expression of the cultural zeitgeist: "A city in the desert. A culture of possibility. A network of dreamers and doers."[3]

The Burning Man culture is based on ten principles, principles that largely express the contours of the New Copernican sensibility: no boundaries, a priority on experience and participation, expressive individualism, respectful community, autonomous authenticity, oneness with nature, justice, beauty, love, and spirit. Burning Man is more than a fun festival, more than an updated Woodstock. Less a music festival, it's a social experiment and cultural critique.[4] The festival's ten principles were written by Larry Harvey in 2004, after the anarchy of Burning Man in the 1990s required more social structure.

1. *Radical Inclusion.* Anyone may be a part of Burning Man. We welcome and respect the stranger. No prerequisites exist for participation in our community.
2. *Gifting.* Burning Man is devoted to acts of gift giving. The value of a gift is unconditional. Gifting does not contemplate a return or an exchange for something of equal value.
3. *Decommodification.* In order to preserve the spirit of gifting, our community seeks to create social environments that are unmediated by commercial sponsorships, transactions, or advertising. We stand ready to protect our culture

from such exploitation. We resist the substitution of consumption for participatory experience.

4. *Radical Self-reliance.* Burning Man encourages the individual to discover, exercise and rely on his or her inner resources.

5. *Radical Self-expression.* Radical self-expression arises from the unique gifts of the individual. No one other than the individual or a collaborating group can determine its content. It is offered as a gift to others. In this spirit, the giver should respect the rights and liberties of the recipient.

6. *Communal Effort.* Our community values creative cooperation and collaboration. We strive to produce, promote and protect social networks, public spaces, works of art, and methods of communication that support such interaction.

7. *Civic Responsibility.* We value civil society. Community members who organize events should assume responsibility for public welfare and endeavor to communicate civic responsibilities to participants. They must also assume responsibility for conducting events in accordance with local, state and federal laws.

8. *Leaving No Trace.* Our community respects the environment. We are committed to leaving no physical trace of our activities wherever we gather. We clean up after ourselves and endeavor, whenever possible, to leave such places in a better state than when we found them.

9. *Participation.* Our community is committed to a radically participatory ethic. We believe that transformative change, whether in the individual or in society, can occur only through the medium of deeply personal participation. We achieve being through doing. Everyone is invited to work.

Everyone is invited to play. We make the world real through actions that open the heart.

10. *Immediacy.* Immediate experience is, in many ways, the most important touchstone of value in our culture. We seek to overcome barriers that stand between us and a recognition of our inner selves, the reality of those around us, participation in society, and contact with a natural world exceeding human powers. No idea can substitute for this experience.[5]

The exponential growth of Burning Man has led to its detractors and has required more rules. Some question its authenticity today compared to a much looser, wilder, and more dangerous scene in the '90s. But the growth of the festival and the tensions it has inspired make its lessons much more influential within the wider culture. The vision and structure of Burning Man is much more replicable elsewhere.[6] One soon expects to see more filmmaking made with Burning Man as the cultural backdrop. At its best, Burning Man is an experience of liminality, a desire to transcend or find the sacred in the ordinary. Larry Harvey writes, "Were we to remove all soul and all spirit from experience, we would be left with little more than what William James called, 'a cold and a neutral state of intellectual perception.' In such an arid landscape, there would be no urgent meanings, no riveting purposes, and the juice of reality would be squeezed out of the world."[7]

If Burning Man is New Copernicans' most reflective cultural event, then the open immanent social imaginary is their natural habitat. Here is the church's missional front line. If we pay close attention to the world they are now creating in business, education, politics, religion, and philanthropy, we can begin to see the long-term significance of this emerging perspective. New Copernicans are in the process of rethinking their understanding of human society. We are now caught in that brief interlude between the lightning of their insight and the thunder of its implications to cultural institutions. As we touched on before, even now the Olympics and the Republican Party are aware that they face a crisis because of the disaffection of millennials. The evangelical church will follow. So millennials are a benefit to us as observers because their reactions are valuable in determining the ongoing implications of this culture shift.

But it is also a liability that millennials are so native to an open immanent social imaginary. It is such a taken-for-granted reality for them that they are unable to describe it to others or seize the cultural opportunities before them. In most cases millennials only intuit the shift they embody but possess neither the language to express it nor the categories to understand it. The power of culture is the power of defining reality. Without a language to describe their social imaginary, millennials remain at a cultural disadvantage. As we have seen, others will define them for us—ABC's *The Great Indoors*, for example—and most often in ways that distort and alienate them.

One point of confusion in the social imaginaries' terminology is in the word *immanent*, by which Charles Taylor means a form of "secular." As seen on the chart, both New Atheists and New Copernicans are secular in their orientation. James K. A. Smith defines the immanent frame as "a constructed social space that frames our lives entirely within a natural (rather than supernatural) order."[8] However, New Copernicans are secular in a different way than New Atheists.

In Charles Taylor's study of secularity, *A Secular Age,* he explores three uses of the word *secular*: secularism$_1$, secularism$_2$, and secularism$_3$.

1. Secularism$_1$—medieval, one-dimensional perspective (1-D)
2. Secularism$_2$—Enlightenment, two-dimensional perspective (2-D)
3. Secularism$_3$—contemporary, three-dimensional perspective (3-D)[9]

What we are suggesting is that the New Copernican frame shift is the move from secularism$_2$ (Enlightenment) to secularism$_3$ (post-postmodern). Rather than thinking of a "secular" age (secularism$_3$) as synonymous with unbelief, Taylor suggests that it is now best understood as contested ways of apprehending reality.[10]

In the medieval age secularism$_1$ refers to worldly vocations; for example, farmers were secular and priests were religious. Secularism$_1$ had to do with one's position or status within a generally unified and transcendent understanding of society. The medieval use of *secular* did not have any negative religious connotation. For Christian and non-Christian alike, the lordship of Christ was assumed within the medieval world. Everyone assumed they were living within a larger spiritual reality under a religious canopy, in which they merely served different functions—farmers being secular, priests being religious.

This changed in early modernity and into the Enlightenment. During this period, the secular became what Taylor calls secularism$_2$. Assuming that secular reason was unbiased, rational, and opposed to tradition (the *ancien régime*), secularism$_2$ pitted reason against faith and science against religion. This either/or binary framing of ideas came to shape debates about science and religion. This view dominated until recently and is evidenced in the public controversy surrounding New Atheism. The secularization thesis when presented as a "subtraction story"—"tales of enlightenment and progress and maturation that see the emergence of modernity and 'the secular' as shucking the detritus of belief and superstition"—is not correct, which opens the door to secularism$_3$.[11]

What we experience in secularism$_3$, rather than an antipathy toward faith, is a renewed openness and explosion of many modes of believing, all of which are contested and held with a more humble open hand. The either/or dichotomies of secularism$_2$ are rejected for the both/and framing of secularism$_3$. Seth Godin counsels, "In a world where nuance, uncertainty, and shades of grey are ever more common, becoming comfortable with ambiguity is one of the most valuable skills you can acquire. If you view your job as taking multiple choice tests, you will never be producing as much value as you are capable of. . . . Life is an essay, not a Scantron machine."[12] So a secular$_3$ age does not entail the rise of atheism and unbelief but instead the rise of cross-pressured belief, where belief and doubt are fused comfortably together. Smith explains: "The 'salient feature of the modern cosmic imaginary' or cultural narrative that Taylor highlights 'is. that it has opened space in which people can wander between and around all these options without having to land clearly and definitely in any one.'"[13] Seekers, explorers, and pilgrims all. The New Copernican shift is a shift from secularism$_2$ to secularism$_3$. This is the problem with most of the research on religious nones: it posits the data within a secularism$_2$ frame and thereby misses the point. Secularism$_2$ and the assumptions of the Enlightenment from which it emerged is the main foil in the book's argument. If New Copernicans are post-secular, then what we mean is that they are post-secularism$_2$.[14]

There are various ways researchers have tried to categorize open immanents. Sociologist Nancy Ammerman places them in three spiritual packages: (1) theistic, (2) nontheistic, and (3) ethical.[15]

Theologian Linda Mercadante puts them in five categories: (1) dissenters—those who stay away from institutional religion often because they were hurt by it; (2) casuals—spiritual practices were primarily functional as is sometimes seen in discussions about mindfulness; (3) explorers—people with a spiritual wanderlust who are tourists of other religions; (4) seekers—people genuinely looking for a spiritual home often reclaiming an earlier religious identity; and (5) immigrants—those who have moved to a new spiritual land.[16] When Mercadante examined the "spiritual but not religious" group as a whole, she did not find an eclectic New Age sensibility among them as some might have suspected. She found instead a post-Christian spirituality. She summarizes her findings as such:

> They virtually all rejected religious or salvationary exclusivism and championed an internal rather than transcendent "locus of authority." Almost all embraced a liberative ethos—especially in gender and sexual orientation issues—rather than accepting older role-restrictive teachings. Most had a belief in "Universal Truth" as well as affirming the essential similarity of all religions. Most downplayed religious commitment. Many had a decidedly therapeutic orientation to spiritual practice. They also demonstrated a positive-thinking ethos or conviction that one's ideas create one's reality. Most soundly rejected the idea of "sin." The vast majority used spiritual experience as a touchstone and often saw nature as a source or mediator of spiritual feelings.[17]

This is not pantheism and it is not orthodox theism; rather it is a kind of halfway position between pantheism and progressive Christianity. Clearly, we are not moving toward no religion but toward a post-secular spirituality. Mercadante concludes that many of the "spiritual but not religious" that she interviewed want "a resacralization of the world. They want to see and experience the sacred in more areas of life. They want a spirituality that is vital and personal."[18]

A more recent study of these believers was conducted by Public Religion Research Institute: "Exodus: Why Americans Are Leaving Religion—and Why They're Unlikely to Come Back."[19] They categorize these believers in three groups: (1) 59 percent rejectionist—angry; (2) 22 percent apatheists—don't care; and (3) 18 percent unattached believers—personally important. Overall the religiously unaffiliated Americans are significantly younger than religiously affiliated Americans, with more than a third coming from those under the age of thirty. From this data it is evident that the church itself is the source of many of these problems and attitudes, especially when three-quarters of those classified religious nones grew up in the church.[20] In many cases, their rejection of the church is not a rejection of religion or faith, but a rejection of the 2-D either/or framing represented by the closed transcendent perspective.

In many cases they are angry and suspicious, but increasingly New Copernicans are intrigued by a faith that is more thoughtful and humane: a New Copernican spirituality. New Copernicans are haunted by doubt in their secularity—as James K. A. Smith puts it, "the doubter's doubt is faith."[21] They have a nagging sense of incompleteness, a fear of missing out. The Harris Interactive Eventbrite study found that nearly seven in ten millennials experience the fear of missing out.[22] As one millennial blogger said crassly, "My general rule of thumb: you don't have to believe in everything, but don't f—k with it, just in case."[23] This fear drives them to show up, share, and engage. They are explorers of a larger sphere of meaning, the hope for another world.

New Copernicans represent the cultural front line and the greatest opportunity for the church. But the church will need to learn how to relate to their dominant seven characteristics and appeal to their four spiritual on-ramps to be taken seriously by them and to be useful spiritual pilgrims with them as open transcendent apprentices of Jesus.

TAKEAWAYS FROM CHAPTER TWELVE

- New Copernicans need no warning of the coming shift, as they already embody it.
- Burning Man is a reflection of the New Copernican frame shift in its pure form.
- There are three historical stages to the meaning of the word *secular*.
- The New Copernican frame shift is a transition from secularity$_2$ to secularity$_3$.
- Religious nones need to be seen as a growth in secularity$_3$.
- New Copernican spirituality is not an eclectic New Age but a post-Christian spirituality.

DISCUSSION QUESTIONS FOR CHAPTER TWELVE

- How are Christian millennials often a distortion from an ideal New Copernican?
- What are your attitudes toward the Burning Man Festival? Do you know anyone who has gone?

- What is the difference between secularity$_2$ and secularity$_3$? Have you observed this difference among your friends?
- What do you think it means to be an open transcendent apprentice of Jesus?

THIRTEEN

HUMILITY IN THEOLOGY

The missional task for the church is one of addition, not subtraction. The hauntedness of New Copernicans can be affirmed as a viable on-ramp for further conversation and exploration. Their hidden aspirations as well as the larger designs of reality point to another world. In fact, they point to a personal universe rooted in the reality of love.[1]

If we are going to be useful partners in the pilgrimages of New Copernicans, we will first need to become the kind of people who reflect this larger reality of love. There will need to be a gentleness, flexibility, patience, winsomeness, and openness that have not marked many believers. Richard Rohr cautions, "If you have, in fact, deepened and grown 'in wisdom, age, and grace' (Luke 2:52), you are able to be patient, inclusive, and understanding of all previous stages. . . . The 'adepts' in all religions are always forgiving, compassionate, and radically inclusive. They do not create enemies, and they move beyond the boundaries of their own 'starter group' while still honoring them and making use of them."[2] This is a good summary of the much-needed open attitude.

To be this kind of person, we do not need to know all the answers to all the questions. As we have seen, for New Copernicans the cognitive and intellectual takes a back seat to the relational and the existential. Here EQ trumps IQ. Empathy and mere presence is more helpful than somehow commanding the heights of knowledge. This is not to imply that knowledge is not important. It is. It's just not the first thing. For left-brain–oriented evangelicals, we will have to overemphasize the poetic to get some measure of balance.

What we mean by *addition* is that your relationship with Jesus—participation in the resources of the kingdom of God—builds on your longing for love, justice, beauty, and spirit. It is not anything other than what you are longing for; it is its fulfillment. C. S. Lewis counsels,

> If a man diligently followed his desire, pursuing the false objects until their falsity appeared and then resolutely abandoning them, he must come at last into the clear knowledge that the human soul was made to enjoy some object that is never fully given—nay, cannot even be imagined as given—in our present mode of subjective and spatio-temporal existence. . . . The dialectic of Desire, faithfully followed, would retrieve all mistakes, head you off from all false paths, and force you not to propound, but to live through, a sort of ontological proof.[3]

Lewis argues for a "lived dialectic," a pilgrimage where learning is experiential. Evangelicals tend to think that the Bible alone will guide you home. Few are aware that for many New Copernicans reading the Bible only adds to one's problems of faith. Mike McHargue observes, "More than anything else, it was reading my Bible that had turned me into an atheist."[4] Lewis says a pagan life well lived with brutal honesty will bring you back to the church; the pagan's pilgrimages are not in vain. Lewis observes, "That is the definition of a Pagan—a man so travelling that if all goes well he arrives at Mother Kirk's chair and is carried over the gorge. I saw it happen myself."[5]

If we think of faith as a pilgrimage rather than a light switch, we'll be in a much better place to assist New Copernicans in their spiritual seeking.[6] There are certain characteristics of open transcendent believers. They have a combination of intellectual humility combined with deep spiritual mysticism. There is immediacy to their experience of God that is often combined with a scientific inquisitiveness.

I owe much of my insight into New Copernicans to noted philanthropist Sir John Templeton, who modeled these characteristics, especially late in his life. He is an exemplar of an open transcendent believer. He is hard to put into traditional theological boxes, partially because he believed that the knowledge of God destroys all these boxes. A traditional Presbyterianism, an Eastern panentheism, and an inter-faith Unity Church influenced his views. He was also a strong supporter of the sciences and believed that it might very well be possible to create a "general unified theory" of reality that combines the best of scientific thinking with the deepest religious thinking. Stephen Post describes him as a "scientific mystic," which, of course, puts him in the same company as Albert Einstein. His mysticism was not in the subjective therapeutic direction, but in a science that believed that reality itself was infused by and held together through the spiritual. For Sir John, Paul's statement in Athens—"In him we live and move and have our being" (Acts 17:28)—was not a disconnected dualist spiritual statement, but a statement about the very nature of reality, the very reality that science explores.[7]

One also sees this combination of intellectual humility, experiential mysticism, and scientific inquisitiveness in Mike McHargue, aka "Science Mike." His podcast, *The Liturgist*, is a case study in reaching New Copernicans. Few do it better. His own spiritual trajectory followed that of C. S. Lewis, though in his case with a little less dabbling in Romanticism and the Occult.[8]

If one follows the outline of the four operative social imaginaries there are only three possible trajectories of spiritual pilgrimage if one starts as a closed transcendent, which I describe as (1) round the horn, (2) oblique, and (3) right turn.

FOUR SOCIAL IMAGINARIES
Three Paths of Pilgrimage

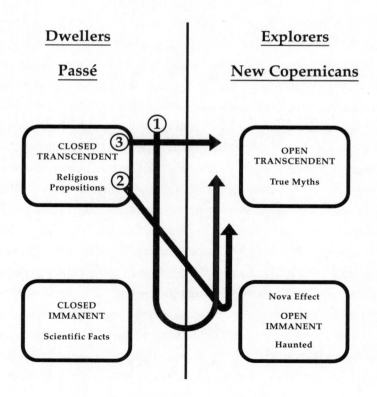

THREE PATHS OF PILGRIMAGE

1. Round the Horn: Closed Transcendent to Closed Immanent to Open Immanent to Open Transcendent

This is, sadly, the most common trajectory. Often the forward trajectory is stunted because of anger toward the church. We should rejoice when people like Rachel Held Evans and Frank Schaeffer maintain some connection with the church after all that they have been through. This is also the trajectory of Mike McHargue, Christian Wiman, and C. S. Lewis.

2. Oblique: Closed Transcendent to Open Immanent to Open Transcendent

This is less common, but is also an approach probably best suited to New Copernicans. Often they will be saved from an atheistic turn by involvement in social justice or art.[9] They typically will move from an orthodox evangelical position to a more progressive Christianity in the process. This may be an easier move to make from liberal Christianity. I suspect that many participants at the Wild Goose Festival—"an art, music, and story-driven transformational experience grounded in faith-inspired social justice"—have this life experience and spiritual journey.[10]

3. Right Turn: Closed Transcendent to Open Transcendent

This is the rarest and perhaps the most costly and jarring spiritual transition. Usually there is an animating event—a crisis of faith or a broken world experience—that precipitates the move. There is usually blood in the water. We should be particularly gentle with folks who have gone through this process. This is the story theologian Peter Enns depicted in his books *The Bible Tells Me So* and *The Sin of Certainty*.

There are obviously those who arrived first at an open transcendent perspective. But these are not those who typically were spiritually formed within the evangelical church. It commonly emerges out of Anglicans, Catholics, and Orthodox Christians. Krista Tippett is certainly a powerful spokesperson for an open transcendent position through her NPR radio broadcast, *On Being*.[11] She came to this view from a Baptist background mediated by a Yale Divinity School degree.

To become an open transcendent believer will mean abandoning the need to be always right, acknowledging one's limits and brokenness, and placing oneself on the dusty road with other pilgrims of all stripes, willing to learn from their pain and joys. It will mean suffering and walking with a limp. It will require becoming a poet. Modern Orthodox saint Porphyrios of Kavsokalyvia put it best when he wrote, "Whoever wants to become a Christian must first become a poet."[12] Spiritual openness demands a right-brained approach to reality; music precedes language. And he quickly adds that the way to become a poet is through suffering. Suffering has a way of winnowing out the pretense, arrogance, and self-confidence that is the greatest barrier to authenticity. This is the "further journey" that Father Richard Rohr calls us to in *Falling Upward*.[13]

If we are willing to embrace this spiritual journey in order to become that kind of person, we'll be well on our way to reaching New Copernicans. In the end there is not a recipe or church program that will do. It is finally about being a certain kind of person. It's the kind of person we see in Sir John Templeton, C. S. Lewis, Parker Palmer, Brennan Manning, Dallas Willard, Krista Tippett, Richard Rohr, and the Dalai Lama.[14]

We cannot effectively reach New Copernicans without first working to become a certain kind of person, the kind of person characterized above.

TAKEAWAYS FROM CHAPTER THIRTEEN

- Being a certain kind of person is more important than developing new programs.
- We need to engage the "dialectic of desire."
- Open transcendent believers have a nonjudgmental combination of intellectual humility and deep spiritual mysticism.
- There are three possible trajectories of growth, each with their own challenges and opportunities: round the horn, oblique, and right turn.
- To become an open transcendent believer will mean abandoning the need to be always right, acknowledging one's limits and brokenness, and placing oneself with other pilgrims willing to learn from their pain and joys.

DISCUSSION QUESTIONS FOR CHAPTER THIRTEEN

- What is required for the church to be effective with New Copernicans?
- Why do evangelicals downplay the importance of desire?
- Have you met a person who embodies the characteristics of an open transcendent believer? What made this person different?
- What does this mean: "Whoever wants to become a Christian must first become a poet"? Does this make sense to you?

PART FOUR

THE FRAME SHIFT IN FOCUS

In responding to the pan-pan warning, the church will learn much from observing New Copernicans as they intuitively embrace the frame shift. There are seven characteristics of millennial New Copernicans: secular, open, cross-pressured, experiential, relational, authentic, and haunted. What we will find is that an adequate response to New Copernicans is simply a renewed commitment to becoming authentic apprentices of Jesus. This section will highlight each characteristic in terms of what the church can do to respond specifically to each characteristic. It clarifies our view of the ice field—the frame shift—we are entering.

FOURTEEN

SECULAR

EMBRACING THE STARDUST

Nobody likes to be reduced to a list, no one more than millennials. And yet day after day marketing agencies and branding gurus print lists of millennial characteristics. Generally, they are behavioral in orientation and framed by various consumer choices. They don't get at the "why" behind their "what," and as such are not very helpful. More useful is to try to get at their mind-set, the way they think about the nature of the good life. Over the course of the following chapters I will describe seven characteristics of this emerging social imaginary exemplified by New Copernicans.

We will also look at each as a way of expressing how the church should respond to them. My assumption is that if we take these characteristics seriously and respond to them appropriately, New Copernicans will receive us much more warmly. As one Burner said to an Episcopal priest at Burning Man, "Thank you for giving me faith again in faith."[1]

The first of these characteristics is *secular.* As we have examined in previous chapters, New Copernicans live their lives within an immanent frame: that is, they assume that their lives can be lived successfully within the natural order without any reference to the transcendent or God. The idea of God is not an operational part of their day-to-day life assumptions, and it is not a part of their vision for the good life.

But as we have indicated, their secularity is not like that of the past. It's not like the binary 2-D either/or assumptions of the Enlightenment. It's rather a complex 3-D both/and perspective that in no way delimits the possibility of transcendence. So we have this odd mixture of God not being a daily operational reality and at the same time not excluded. New Copernicans are both functional atheists and potential spiritual mystics. Consequently, secularism today cannot be seen as synonymous with unbelief. Rather it is best seen as an open but contesting way of apprehending reality. This leads to the Nova Effect.

A supernova is a rare astronomical event that occurs in the last evolutionary stages of a massive star, whose dramatic and catastrophic destruction is marked by one final titanic explosion and visible bright light. Only three supernovas have been observed in our Milky Way galaxy, though others have been observed in other galaxies. In certain views of cosmology, the carbon, hydrogen, and oxygen that make up your DNA came from the crucible of a dying star. Every atom in your body was once stardust. In this sense, the Nova Effect is both a metaphor and potentially more than one.

The Nova Effect is "the explosion of different options for belief and meaning in a secular$_3$ age, produced by the concurrent cross pressures of our history."[2] By "cross pressure" we mean the awareness of various spiritual options and the feeling of being caught between the echo of transcendence and the drive toward a self-sufficient naturalistic life.[3]

I had dinner recently in New York with a Scottish filmmaker who grew up in a totally secular family. The only scar he has from his exposure to British Anglicanism in boarding school is "boredom." His spiritual journeying has taken him deep into Tibetan Buddhism. He had no patience with the New Atheist secularism so prevalent in England. He likewise is skeptical of easy pop New Age answers to deep philosophical and religious questions. He believes that one's spiritual journey should be rooted in a tradition larger than the confines of one's own ego. He was the poster child of the Nova Effect, being immersed in an open immanent social imaginary: skeptical and believing at the same time.

This proliferation of options for meaning may be religious or atheistic. The Nova Effect does not in any way predispose a person to move toward transcendence. But even so, "potentially more than a metaphor" suggests that in a deep cosmic manner there is an underlying unity to the Nova Effect. There is something common behind all of these expressions of belief and meaning, just as all our atoms once came from a dying star. This unity is not found in belief but in longing; we find an essential unity here in our deepest human desires and longings.

By and large, we have not been taught to think in this manner. Framed by a 2-D secularism$_2$ perspective, we tend to see everything as a war of ideas rather than a fusion of longings. We need to take this Nova Effect seriously. This is the cultural milieu of our ministry, an eclectic ecumenism of longing.

This means that we need to stop turning our attention to the likes of the New Atheists. We need to focus our attention on the open immanent social imaginary. This will require substantial retooling of our ministerial preparation. It will mean taking desires more seriously than ideas, to affirm that we are lovers before thinkers, bodies before minds.[4] Much of our evangelism and apologetics will need to be rethought. We are playing Hearts not Spades, and we will need to learn the apologetics of the imagination that places a priority on story and music.[5]

We will also need to learn how to move people from accepting "myths" to acknowledging "myths that are true"—enabling people to move from Joseph Campbell to Jesus Christ.[6] In some evangelical circles, we freak out over the very notion of myths. We can't even get to the general acceptance of the universality and power of myths—the collective unconscious. We will need a robust understanding of spiritual archetypes in order to make connections to biblical theology. We will not be able to unmask the gods without a greater appreciation for and knowledge of these universal myths.[7] This will require a nonjudgmental understanding of secular myths with their variety of neo-pagan expressions. It is significant that the most influential myth writer of our day is Neil Gaiman, whose novel *American Gods*, which is being released in 2017 as a cable TV series, was the centerpiece of the grand hall at Comic-Con in 2016.[8] Comic-Con is an annual comic book convention that draws 130,000 fans of the genres—graphic novels, superhero movies, video games, animation—that comprise fantasy culture. Next to Burning Man, Comic-Con is a zeitgeist cultural event. To meaningfully embrace the mission field of the American Nova Effect, it will take a generous understanding of the signals of transcendence and common grace.[9]

If we are to understand and appreciate the Nova Effect (which does not mean agreeing with it), we will need to be sympathetic to animism and pantheism, what Lewis called man's "natural religion," or neo-paganism. We will need to become familiar with the "the more-than-human world" depicted in the spirituality of deep ecology.[10] Lutheran theologians Carl Braaten and Robert Jenson note, "Neo-paganism refers to modern variations of the ancient belief of pre-Christian mystery religions that a divine spark or seed is innate in the individual human soul. Salvation consists of liberating the divine essence from all that prevents its true self-expression. The way of salvation is to turn inward and 'to get in touch with oneself,' as people say today."[11] This kind of religious belief is off-putting to many evangelicals, but it should not be.

Clotilde Morhan, Bay Area writer and author of *Paganism and the Conversion of C.S. Lewis,* writes, "It was pagan mythological literature, permeated as it was with the intuitive belief in the supernatural, which set Lewis searching for God. . . . Pagan literature—Greek myths, the sagas and eddas of Norse mythology and the epics of classical antiquity—acted upon him as a *preparatio evangelica.*"[12] Can we, too, learn to celebrate neo-pagan spirituality in our culture as an improvement over a world without windows?[13] An awareness of gods or spirits is far better than a scorched earth naturalism and is far closer to the gospel.

Neo-paganism is the spiritual voice of popular culture. Cultural critic Camille Paglia writes, "If you look at it from my perspective, popular culture is an eruption of paganism—which is also a sacred style. . . . We are steeped in idolatry. The sacred is everywhere. I don't see any secularism. We've returned to the age of polytheism. It's a rebirth of pagan gods. Judeo-Christianity never defeated paganism, but rather drove it underground."[14] Now that Judeo-Christianity is in cultural decline, however, what was once underground is now resurfacing as a popular means of spiritual communion.

Such reactions are an illustration of Christianity's own complicity with the spirit and structures of modernity. Evangelicals prefer the practical atheism of capitalism and the techno-humanism of scientism to a belief system that sees spirits in trees or rocks. We would do well to reread C. S. Lewis: "Christians and pagans had much more in common with each other than either has with a post-Christian. The gap between those who worship different gods is not so wide as that between those who worship and those who do not."[15] For many, neo-paganism is a way back to spiritual reality. We need to celebrate and appreciate this neo-pagan cultural turn.[16]

How, then, should the church respond to the growth of neo-paganism?

First, we must humanize neo-pagan believers. We must get to know them as individual people and listen to their stories. There are many points of potential connection. Dallas Willard wrote that everything living draws its life from an environment larger than and other than itself.[17] Pierre Teilhard de Chardin is attributed to have said, "We are not human beings having a spiritual experience, but spiritual beings having a human experience."[18] We are made for another world, as Lewis puts it. Around these themes an orthodox Christian and a neo-pagan can have a fruitful conversation about connection, love, and the nature of the universe.

Second, we must recognize that the growth of neo-paganism is an indictment against the church. We must repent of our own spiritual and cultural culpability rather than reproach those who are attracted to a vital, nature-centric spirituality, which is in their mind more spiritually animated, more holistic, more experiential, and more compassionate in practice than the cognitively truncated, privately marginalized, politically judgmental religion of many evangelicals. Catholic philosopher Thomas Molnar states,

"The spiritual vacuum that prevails in modern society with the complicity of the church makes it quite natural for people to turn to pagan religions and the occult, even as two thousand years ago people turned from paganism to more emotion-laden creeds and to Christianity."[19] Evangelical churches are too often business enterprises before they are spiritual communities—pastors are CEOs rather than spiritual guides. Various forms of neo-paganism are resurfacing as the church's influence on culture has weakened in American culture. We need a renewed emphasis on the reality of the living presence of Christ and nature as a portal to transcendence.

Third, we will not have anything to say to the neo-pagan if we don't have a biblically strengthened view of creation and our stewardship of it. We do not worship nature as the neo-pagan, but we are obligated to respect, honor, and husband it. Again and again there is evidence of the church's complicity in the commodification of nature. Crippled with a truncated two-chapter gospel (fall/redemption), we have a weak appreciation for creation and our essential co-redemptive role in it.[20] We demythologize the poetry of the Psalms, which speaks of nature created to give glory to the Creator. Instead we use nature for our own glory, totally divorcing it from its creational intent. Evangelical attitudes toward climate change are often a conversation stopper. So, too, are our cavalier attitudes toward animals and other sentient beings.[21] Eye-rolling environmental or animal activists are not going to help evangelicals move the conversation forward. It's not just New Copernicans who groan at our attitudes towards nature; so does creation itself (Rom. 8:22).

Finally, we need to appropriate the reality of the incarnate Jesus in our daily lives. Theology that fails to be embodied in daily life fails to be theology rightly understood. Christians need to move beyond cognitive theological abstractions to a resacralized daily existence in which the Unseen Real has more weight and immediacy than anything else.[22]

The power and impact of the L'Abri community in Switzerland was not merely the spiritual and philosophical wisdom of Francis Schaeffer; rather it was the mere fact that as a community they counted on God for everything.[23] Incarnation was not simply a theological premise, but a methodological practice. What does it mean for us to model Christ's incarnation? At the very least it means a visible reliance on the reality of God in our lives.

Neo-paganism will be a growing challenge to the church. It is also an opportunity. It calls apprentices of Jesus to recommit our practice once again to biblical first things. Ironically, the secular characteristic of New Copernicans calls us to a renewed sacralization of our faith. The secular tendency of New Copernicans requires us to be more spiritual. There is something in their spiritual longing that calls us back to Christ. The Nova Effect reminds us again of the source of our spiritual being. The practical takeaway is that the church needs to focus on the Nova Effect, standing in the midst of the cultural front line once again.

TAKEAWAYS FROM CHAPTER FOURTEEN

- The seven characteristics of New Copernicans are a list of "whys" not "whats." The goal is to get at a mind-set, not behaviors or consumer choices.
- New Copernicans are functional atheists and potential spiritual mystics.
- New Copernicans have created the Nova Effect: the

explosion of different options for belief and meaning in a secular$_3$ age, produced by the concurrent cross pressures of history.

- Our human unity is found in our longings, not our beliefs.
- Evangelicals need to focus their attention on those who have an open immanent social imaginary, which is the missional front line.
- We need to learn how to move people from myths to myths that really happened.
- Evangelicals need a greater understanding of and appreciation for neo-paganism.
- New Copernicans require us to resacralize our faith.

DISCUSSION QUESTIONS FOR CHAPTER FOURTEEN

- How have you noticed the Nova Effect in your community? Can you provide examples from your health food store or yoga studio bulletin board?
- What are the challenges and opportunities of neo-paganism?
- What are the most obvious disconnects that our neo-pagan neighbors have with us that we should overcome? Where do we connect?

FIFTEEN

EXPLORERS

MUD ON YOUR SHOES

The second characteristic of New Copernicans is openness, the move from dweller to explorer, from someone who presumes to have a corner on truth to one who is continually learning and growing. This shift in attitude, which is the main focus of this book, is often very difficult for evangelicals. But if we are to enter into a shared pilgrimage with New Copernicans, then we need to get off our soapbox and into the dirt, mud, and messiness of the pilgrim's path. We must hold in our minds the picture of being together on a shared pilgrimage to a yet undeclared or realized destination.

By using this metaphor of shared sacred pilgrimage, I am not suggesting all spiritual paths lead magically to the same place. I am simply suggesting that what is as important as an imagined future destination is the quality of our encounter on the path in the present. *It is the journey that will change us.* The problem with the traditional view of evangelism is that it falsely bifurcates destination and journey, placing almost exclusive emphasis on the destination with no reference or regard for the necessity, beauty, immediacy, and meaning of the journey. Our picture of conversion is of a light switch—once again binary—rather than an ongoing pilgrimage: a potentially messy and long process, as in "continue to work out your salvation with fear and trembling" (Phil. 2:12). Creating meaningful, love-filled moments along the journey is just as important as delivering the friend to the destination . . . if that ever happens. We share together the mythic hero's journey, the Greek epic, and the pilgrim's progress. It is in this shared experience of spiritual companionship on an open-ended spiritual adventure that God works in the pilgrim's life, my own and that of my fellow sojourner.

Pilgrimage, in the ancient sense, is not a common experience today. Wikipedia defines *pilgrimage* as "a journey or search for moral or spiritual significance. Typically, it is a journey to a shrine or other location of importance to a person's beliefs and faith, although sometimes it can be a metaphorical journey into someone's own beliefs."[1] Like the various stories told in *The Canterbury Tales,* there is much to be learned from each person's story.

Just as it is emblematic of modern New Copernicans' sensibilities, the annual Burning Man Festival is also a pilgrimage. The burning of the temple—which cannot be understood as anything other than a sacred space that draws our own struggles and ambiguities into a meaning larger than ourselves—at Burning Man is met with silent reverence by the tens of thousands who witness it on the final night of the festival. There is holiness there—or in Burning Man parlance, "irreverent sacredness."

To view life as a pilgrimage is to understand journey as a liminal space. The word *liminality* comes from the Latin *limen,* meaning "a threshold." The pilgrimage is a transformational space between a real known world and an unknown imaginary world of risk and possibility.

Consider four films that make pilgrimage a metaphor for life: *Into the Wild* (2007), *Eat, Pray, Love* (2010), *Wild* (2014), and *A Walk in the Woods* (2015). In each film, which character is the most beneficial companion on the journey? What were his or her characteristics? What was it about the personal encounter that made it meaningful? What can we learn from this? Most of us need to get off our self-righteous soapboxes and stop preaching. We need to join others on the damp and cold trail and simply listen to the stories of others. There we will find wisdom for our own journey. We need to stop trying to be the guru, shaman, or spiritual know-it-all to others. Rather we need to get down in the muck with them, those who with us are trying to muddle through life with some measure of personal integrity and open search for meaning. As one friend said to me, "I'll love you to heaven or I'll love you to hell. You can count on me loving you either way, the whole way."[2]

To be effective with New Copernicans one must get out of the transaction business and get into the business of personal presence. A young idealistic British seeker joined Mother Teresa for a summer. Day after day he attended the sick and dying on the streets of Calcutta. At the end of the summer he complained about not feeling like he had made any difference. She smiled and said simply, "You were there."[3] Is it enough for us to be truly there in another person's life? It may be. Malcolm Muggeridge is quoted by Gregory Wolfe, "'Mother Teresa is a living conversation' and simply to be near her was to be converted."[4]

Too often the church is in the transaction business, whether it's evangelism or church growth, seemingly involved but cut off from the potential for presence. Can we learn to listen to the stories of others like those shared by the pilgrims in *The Canterbury Tales*, and simply honor the integrity of their story and their courage in pilgrimage?

There are lessons the contemporary church can learn about pilgrimage from ancient Celtic Christianity. The Celts were explorers. Pilgrimage and exploration were in their ethos and central to their storytelling. This interest was not island-bound wanderlust or curious tourist fascination. Exploration became a central spiritual practice given the Latin name *peregrinatio*, which means the "voluntary abandonment of home and kin for ascetic purposes."[5] The dynamic of these pilgrimages was that there was no known destination when one set out on the journey. The spiritual purpose was simply to trust the process, to see where winds and waves took you. It has the same kind of open-endedness seen in God's charge to Abram, "Go from your country, your people and your father's household to the land I will show you" (Gen. 12:1). The journey was the thing, not the destination. Esther de Waal, one of Celtic Christianity's preeminent scholars, reminds us, "I shall not find Christ at the end of the journey unless he accompanies me along the way."[6]

The most famous and revered Celtic explorer is Brendan the Navigator, the Celtic monk who is supposed to have sailed from Ireland to America five hundred years before Columbus. In 1976 adventurer Tim Severin built a traditional Irish curragh, a thirty-two-foot, two-mast, wooden-framed boat covered in oiled skins. He completed a voyage to Newfoundland from Ireland, proving that the ancient tale could have been possible. More difficult than completing this epic voyage is recapturing this ancient attitude. It requires seeing oneself and others as being on a shared spiritual pilgrimage, providing focused attention so as to be fully present with the other person, and trusting the Holy Spirit in that moment.

Look at your feet. Is there mud on your shoes?

TAKEAWAYS FROM CHAPTER FIFTEEN

- The move from dweller to explorer is the second characteristic of New Copernicans and is the most difficult characteristic for evangelicals to identify with even as it is perhaps the most important.
- Creating meaningful love-filled moments along others' spiritual journeys is as important as delivering them to a final destination.
- To be effective with New Copernicans one must get out of the transaction business and into the intimacy of personal presence.

DISCUSSION QUESTIONS FOR CHAPTER FIFTEEN

- Why is the shift from closed to open so difficult for evangelical leaders? What special challenges do they face in making this shift?
- What attitude is suggested by describing one's faith journey as a "shared sacred pilgrimage"?
- How does this understanding of pilgrimage change our views of evangelism?
- How does one create meaningful love-filled moments? Do you have relationships characterized by that?

SIXTEEN

CROSS-PRESSURED BELIEFS

DARK NIGHT OF THE SOUL

The third characteristic of New Copernicans is their experience of cross-pressured beliefs. This is the result of living in a hyperpluralistic world: the ongoing sense of dissonance that there are other options to one's beliefs and that one is caught between an immanent life and a transcendent longing. The consequence of this cross-pressured experience is double-edged, simultaneously containing liabilities and benefits, as it reduces the plausibility of beliefs currently held and creates an openness to new beliefs and experiences. To put it bluntly, no one today believes what they believe in the same manner as they once believed. The innocence of naïve belief is gone, dashed on the rocks of diversity—diversity of options for belief and diversity of believers. A person whose diet was limited to bread and water now faces a fifty-foot culinary smorgasbord. Over time, this largess will change his or her approach toward food . . . just as it has done to his or her beliefs and believing. James K. A. Smith observes,

Charles Taylor not only explains *un*belief in a secular age; he also emphasizes that even belief is changed in our secular age. There are still believers who believe the same things as their forebears 1,500 years ago; but *how* we believe has changed. Thus faith communities need to ask: How does this change in the "conditions" of belief impact the way we proclaim and teach the faith? How does this impact faith formation? How should this change the propagation of the faith for the next generation?[1]

The operative takeaway for the church's response to the cross-pressured character of New Copernicans is personal vulnerability. We will have to acknowledge the cross-pressured nature of our own evangelical beliefs. We will not be able to connect with authenticity unless we are able to express the contingent nature of our own convictions.

This means that doubt will need to be given more airtime in church. As long as this remains a taboo topic, New Copernican believers will not be able to identify with the seemingly false pretense of our religious experience. When we preach, we need to acknowledge how strange some of the Bible seems to modern ears. Glossing over these texts with a too-pious-by-half spirituality will only serve to move others' doubts towards skepticism.

Evangelical pastors have been tempted to become celebrity exemplars of certainty. A benefit of Catholicism is that they do not saint Christians until after they are dead, but Protestant beatification often happens as a result of a person's celebrity status within the church or consumer market while they are still living. Life-sized cardboard cutouts of the pastor in the church narthex is a sure sign of such hubris. Portland pastor A. J. Swoboda criticizes this practice: "We don't actually allow preachers the space or freedom to teach from the textbook of their wandering experiences. . . . Those in my trade have become certainty machines, pumping out a steady stream of safe truths meeting the emerging market of consumer Christians who yearn for cliché more than Christ."[2] Megan DeFranza laments, "I can recall less than a handful of preachers able to speak into my experience as a follower of The Way with questions unsatisfied by the usual answers."[3] She asks these pressing questions:

Is it even possible to be a preacher living with hard questions?
Do we still expect our pastors to have the answers?
Are priests allowed to be human?
Are our leaders allowed to keep learning?[4]

This gets to the heart of what we think is the essential aspect of faith: belief or trust? Knowledge or relationship? If we think that the essential task of our sermon is information transfer, we will preach in a certain manner. If, on the other hand, it is connecting our deepest longings with all our brokenness with the risen presence of Christ, it will take our sermons in a different direction. We don't have to be an answer machine to be in love with Jesus; in fact, often it is a hindrance: "For I tell you that unless your righteousness surpasses that of the Pharisees and the teachers of the law, you will certainly not enter the kingdom of heaven" (Matt. 5:20). Ironically, it is often the case that the spiritual vitality of faith decreases while a seminarian is in seminary. Knowledge replaces the relational at a cost.

Here we see again that the appropriate response to the New Copernican sensibility is not a new program, but being a different kind of person. What New Copernicans are looking for is an authentic person who is grounded in a dynamic relationship with Jesus and who is able to connect deeply with the longings and losses of others in a manner that is deeply human. This is not the kind of person formed in a seminary, but formed in the crucible of life. There is something terribly wrong with our churches when we cannot be safe places for unsafe questions, when we have to consistently paper over the cracks in our broken hearts on Sunday morning. Anglican priest David Runcorn laments,

> There is nothing sadder than a Christian fellowship where every song must be victory, every prayer full of faith, every member always smiling and joyful. It is an exhausting pretense to keep up for long, and it condemns those who cannot hide from their fears to further pain of failure and inadequacy. It is actually dishonest. It means that we can never offer our tears as well as our smiles, our questions as well as our certainties, our wounds as well as our victories. It means that we are always keeping Christ out of the very places in our lives where we need him the most— the places of darkness, uncertainties, and fears.[5]

It is not spoken of too loudly in evangelical circles, but many are aware that there is a kind of advanced discipleship graduate school embraced by few known as the "dark night of the soul."[6] It is less a spiritual crisis than a thorough spiritual refining. Persons who have been through this fire are changed. (One thinks of Mother Teresa, who walked in the "dark night" during the final years of her life.) Secondary things are no longer confused as first things. Connection and love predominate. They are "broken world people," and it is these kinds of people that Christ can use with New Copernicans. So we have to ask, "Do you walk with a limp?"

New Copernicans have a highly honed crap detector. We will have to be much more transparent about the nature of belief and the messiness of discipleship if we are to have credibility with New Copernican sensibilities. Some evangelicals were shocked by the revelation of Mother Teresa's long dark night of the soul depicted in her letters,[7] yet her struggle would only serve to confirm her authentic faith in the minds of New Copernican explorers. We must honestly embrace the cross-pressured nature of belief today. We must be able to give voice to our doubts even as we walk in faith. It is true of secular seekers as it is true of religious believers. As Charles Taylor notes, in this sense we are all secular now. However, many evangelicals are unwilling to admit this fact. And once again we find that responding to the New Copernican opportunity will make us more like Jesus.

TAKEAWAYS FROM CHAPTER SIXTEEN

- The third characteristic of New Copernicans is their experience of cross-pressured beliefs. This is the consequence of living in a hyperpluralistic world.
- The operative takeaway for the church to the experience of the cross-pressured character of belief is personal vulnerability.
- Doubt needs to be given more airtime in church.
- Evangelical pastors should not be certainty machines.
- Advanced discipleship includes the experience of the dark night of the soul.

DISCUSSION QUESTIONS FOR CHAPTER SIXTEEN

- How do you experience a cross-pressured reality in your own views?
- How does the cross-pressured nature of belief impact the way we proclaim and teach the faith?
- What are the institutional and structural obstacles to evangelical leaders being more vulnerable?
- What are the characteristics of an authentic person?
- Have you experienced the dark night of the soul? How did it change you?

SEVENTEEN

EXPERIENTIAL

BOUTIQUE HOSPITALITY

The fourth dominant characteristic of New Copernicans is their experiential orientation. While we have spoken of this in chapter 8, let's now look at how this might influence our approach to church.

Consider first how this has influenced the fitness industry. Millennials are leaving large gyms for smaller, themed boutique studios such as Barry's Bootcamp or SoulCycle. Proximity and being in the neighborhood was not enough to keep them there. Size and full-service options was also not a draw. They want a smaller community and personalized attention. Molly Shea writing in the *New York Post*, says, "A decade ago, the fitness industry was dominated by neighborhood gyms and a handful of specialty studios. Now, boutique studios represent a larger-than-ever slice of the fitness pie—42% of the market in 2014, a 100% increase over 2013, according to the International Health, Racquet & Sportsclub Association."[1] We've seen the same trend in big-box retail, where stores such as Target are trying to position themselves as a retail hive of disparate boutiques called "The Shops." It is still not clear whether this concept will be successful, but megachurches should pay close attention to these trends in retail.

Besides smaller community and personalized service, what other aspects are important for a retail experience to be successful? Five come immediately to mind. The experience should be unique (even exotic), consequently memorable, photogenic, sharable, and relational. In effect, an event must be Facebook- or Snapchat-posting worthy. Social media is the means by which experiences are shared relationally and validated personally.

It is also important to reemphasize that events cannot be transactional to be authentic. A transactional relationship has the expectation of something in return, an emphasis on what you get from the relationship. If the event has some other agenda that is not clearly stated at the outset, it will be rejected. In other words, do not offer events to get people to attend your church or to hear an evangelistic message. The event needs to be limited to the integrity of the event itself—the one exception being if the event is being done as a benefit to a social cause.

We should consider doing events simply as a celebration of life, of human flourishing, or good companionship. Having fun with new folks should be enough. As we have mentioned before, *Babette's Feast* is the exemplar. Creativity here is what makes for memorable events.

A friend of mine from Colorado held a series of dinners at his home for invited guests over the course of six months, with each dinner themed on one of the drinks in Tom Standage's *New York Times* best seller, *A History of the World in 6 Glasses*. He brought in chefs, wine sommeliers, craft beer guides, and coffee baristas at each event. The meal was paired with the drink. It was a culinary, historical, and relational stroke of genius. People go out to eat a great deal; this is a dominant pastime of millennials. But too few people—including Christians—actually go the expense and effort to cook in their own kitchen. The options for creativity are endless: meals from all the countries represented in your church, the six regions of Scotch whiskey (if Episcopalian), and so on. Similar creativity can take place around music. Millennials have now created a service to invite gifted classical musicians into one's home for a personalized performance—Groupmuse.[2] Unique, exotic, photogenic, and relational—these are the kinds of experiences that New Copernicans crave.

Effective churches are incorporating these aspects into their worship experience, including St. Lydia's Church in New York. The story of St. Lydia's is compelling in that it addresses the characteristics of New Copernicans highlighted here. St. Lydia's is a dinner church, where the entire service centers on a home-cooked meal. There are not many private places in New York, due to the size of apartments, where people can stage a dinner party—St. Lydia's has created a spiritual third place.[3] They bend over backward to dispel the barriers and hesitations that hip-urban New Yorkers have about church. *The Atlantic* article written about the church was entitled, "The Secret Christians of Brooklyn."[4] They acknowledge that believing in Jesus is countercultural to a New York millennial. St. Lydia's is a progressive church supported by the Lutheran and Episcopal dioceses. They are accepting of all people regardless of their beliefs and backgrounds. Openness is a hallmark of St. Lydia's. Pastor Emily Scott tells people, "I'm not from a scary church," by which she means judgmental.

Jeremiah Sierra, who serves on their Leadership Table, writes,

"As someone with about as much doubt as faith, St. Lydia's fulfilled a need in me to engage with my faith without requiring consent to any particular dogma. My engagement is more kinetic than intellectual. I accept and give gifts with my hands—the gifts of love and grace in the form of bread and wine, a dish passed full of food, peace passed with a handshake or a hug."[5] What creates community is the weekly experience of preparing a meal together and cleaning up afterwards. It is not meal-then-worship or worship-then-meal, but the entire meal is established as the liturgy of worship, a genuine experience of a first-century Eucharistic meal. One starts the meal with strangers and ends the cleanup as friends. Friends, C.S. Lewis reminds us, do not gaze into each other's eyes, but do something together.[6] Perhaps the most legitimate measure of membership is when a visitor posts about St. Lydia's on Facebook for the first time, thereby identifying with the church to their friends. During each service someone tells his or her story, not as a testimony of overcoming faith, but as a travelogue update on a long spiritual pilgrimage sometimes in the valley, sometimes on the mountaintop, most often just in the daily struggle of the climb. Everyone is embraced with respectful listening and acceptance. What one experiences here is a divine encounter shared in a context of relational acceptance watered by a message of grace. The church is very active in art and social justice issues. Many writers and other creatives attend. St. Lydia's is a LGBTQ–accepting church, and they are consequently active in providing care and support for these particular social needs. These efforts reflect their congregation and their location in Brooklyn, and are an authentic on-ramp to further spiritual seeking by all. Barbeques and other kinds of meals can be tried in other locations.

Urban environments like New York can be extremely lonely

places. How are churches an antidote to loneliness? A dinner church is not so threatening and is warmly inviting—beauty, worship, friends, and a home-cooked meal. Here is a church that creates an environment for genuine self-reflection, relational connection, and spiritual exploration. It is not surprising that St. Lydia's does not consider itself as a finished project but an ongoing adventure. Here is what a church by millennials for millennials looks like, one that challenges the status quo but at the same time lifts the historic gospel to new heights. Here is a church that can effectively move open immanent seekers to an open transcendent perspective and a loving encounter with Jesus. They are transformed by the authentic experience of encounter. The same should be seen in our homes. Founder of Ransom Fellowship Denis Haack has said that he wants his home in Rochester to be the "safest place in the city" where he can give the gift of "unhurried time." He writes,

> As Christians we may have all the right theology, the right questions, the defensible answers, but unless we have a place of safety and warmth in which to have relationships with real people, we won't be very effective. Our desire has been to make our home a place of interest and beauty where people could come and know that any sort of question or topic could be addressed. An intimate place where we share needs, music, conversation, and allow the power of God to be demonstrated in ordinary everyday ways. We feel that hospitality is more and more necessary to reach this current generation as an antidote to the brokenness and alienation so many have experienced.[7]

Until we can actualize an ethos of grace that is suffused with beauty and love, skeptical New Copernicans will only be waiting for the other shoe to drop. Our lives, homes, and churches' hospitality should be irresistibly inviting, like the smell of fresh-baked bread and hot chocolate, warm and openhanded to all.

TAKEAWAYS FROM CHAPTER SEVENTEEN

- The fourth characteristic of New Copernicans is their experiential orientation.
- An experience should be unique, memorable, photogenic, sharable, and relational.
- We should do events simply as a celebration of life, of human flourishing, or good companionship.

DISCUSSION QUESTIONS FOR CHAPTER SEVENTEEN

- How does St. Lydia's Church in Brooklyn incorporate these experiential dimensions into its corporate worship?
- How could we make our own homes and churches more experientially oriented? Could they become a local third place?

EIGHTEEN

RELATIONSHIPS

VERBS AND NOUNS

The fifth dominant characteristic of New Copernicans is their priority on relationships. At one level, one could conclude that this is because of their age, and that certainly plays a part, particularly with the ambiguity of the hookup scene and the expectation of delayed marriage, but it is also the result of life mediated through ubiquitous hyperconnectivity. Today a third of all marriages in the U.S. start via an online dating site.[1] The integrative dynamic of smartphones in the lives of New Copernicans cannot be overstated. But before one starts in on a critical tirade against millennials and their overreliance on technology, on the appearance of selfie narcissism, and other general criticism of social media, let me ask: What is wrong with being relationally oriented?

Americans of previous generations have made autonomous individualism synonymous with Americanism—the self-made man, the rugged individualist, the Marlboro Man. Not so much millennials, who are not collectivist in the political or sociological sense, but certainly prioritize relationships with their friends. A core network of friends becomes for many a surrogate family, and being loyal to and supporting this family is paramount.

Once again we see that this assessment is a better understanding of reality. Reality is essentially relational. Deepak Chopra asks provocatively, "Are our genes verbs or nouns?" He states, "There are no nouns in the universe. Everything is a relationship. Nouns are conventions of language. The universe is more music than words. The universe is a verb, a process of ceaseless activity."[2] At its deepest level this is what is meant by New Copernican relationality. It's not simply that they have a lot of friends, that they think collectively, but that they have intuited that all lived experience either moves us toward connecting or disconnecting with the other. Reality is relational and love is at the root of all reality. Of course, Dr. Chopra means for this insight to be taken as an extension of his Hindu pantheism. But this is precisely what Christians mean when we say that we live in a trinitarian universe, that the ceaseless dynamic of loving mutuality of the godhead is at the root of all reality, that we are made in God's image. Jesus prays, "Father, just as you are in me and I am in you. May they also be in us so that the world may believe that you have sent me. I have given them the glory that you gave me, that they may be one as we are one—I in them and you in me" (John 17:21–23).

Take a public policy issue like immigration. What difference does it make if we approach it as a verb instead of a noun? My millennial son, Alex, was a participant in Al Jazeera America's reality TV show *Borderland*. They started in a morgue in Tucson, Arizona, filled with three hundred bodies of illegal immigrants who had died in the American desert nearby. They ripped six name tags off the corpses and then learned their stories and retraced their journeys to the points of their death. Alex followed the footsteps of Maira Zelaya from Usulutan, El Salvador, who died in the desert at the age of thirty-nine. Participants met the deceased's families in various Central American countries, rode atop the freight train ("The Beast" or "Death Train") from Guatemala to the United States border, got their supplies in the border villages whose entire economy is based on human trafficking, crossed the border with armed "coyotes," and after a grueling hike were eventually met by the United States Border Patrol.[3] All of this was captured on film.[4]

To address the immigration problem as a noun is to objectify it in a manner that is bloodless and distant. To address immigration as a verb is to identify with the fear, cold, thirst, hunger, and sore muscles of Maira whose footsteps you are retracing. Alex came away from the experience saying the discussions on public policy have little-to-no relationship with the lived experience of the actual immigrant. Alex is a New Copernican who sees reality as a verb. We have much to learn from him.

The evangelical church specializes in instrumental relationships— using others for our own calculated, even if well-intentioned, ends. Nonmembers are targets of evangelism, for example, and members are targets of service projects or discipleship programs. We don't really know how to be in a relationship without an agenda. Older adults may roll their eyes at young people "hanging out." But isn't this simply being with another person without an agenda, without a timetable, and without a script? New Copernicans demand better relationships.

We need to recapture the Celtic priority of belonging before believing, of building relationships first before demanding creedal affirmation. Even more than providing content, churches need to provide safe places for honest conversations—in effect, an alternative to secular third places.[5] Creating safe places for honest questions is at the heart of the approach taken by Q Place, a non-threatening third place designed to facilitate conversations about God, the Bible, and meaning.[6] Are our churches a place where a nonbeliever would want to belong?

The church has the tendency to see relationships as a noun—Christian or non-Christian—which violates the premise of the relationship. It would help if we would see ourselves as "Christianing" rather than being "a Christian"—a verb not a noun. It's being in a dynamic relationship with Jesus that matters, rather than adhering to a static list of doctrines. The church does not need "friendship evangelism"; rather it needs "friendship friendship"—agenda-free loving and listening. In this regard, the church will always be approached with justifiable suspicion by New Copernicans because this premise has been so routinely violated.

"Nouning" is a precursor to judging. Attitudes of judgment—which are presumed by all nonbelievers of believers—make churches and Christians something to be avoided rather than embraced. Why would a sane person want to be with us? We have to earn the right to be *present*, much less *heard*. Rather than preaching and making ourselves heard, we need to learn to listen more than we speak, and start giving of ourselves, our presence, and our love in a sacrificial manner. It's about being like Jesus.

Tattoos are a useful case study. What is your attitude toward them? Would you get one? What do they mean in the life of the person who has one? Tattoos—once the purview of bikers, punks, and rebellious eighteen-year-olds—have circled back into symbols of wellness and a path to spiritual healing. They are so common among millennials, they are culturally mainstream.[7] Tattoos are a way of immortalizing important aspects of one's personal story. Lars Krutak, a tattoo anthropologist and research associate at the Smithsonian, says, "I cannot think of another medium of personal expression and meaning that is so intimately connected to our bodies and memories. The desire to adorn, commemorate, heal, self-identify, empower, and inscribe personal history via tattoo has always been a part of being human."[8]

Nineteenth-century missionaries discouraged native "practices of disfigurement" when native people converted to Christ. It was a part of their Western colonialist values that got mixed up with their missionary efforts. It is this attitude that needs to be challenged, because it doesn't take the cultural significance of storytelling into account.[9] The power of story, embodiment, identity, and spirituality are connected in the tattooing history and experience. We need to embrace this history and experience as a relational on-ramp to a deeper pilgrimage to Jesus.

Tattoos are a reminder that life is a verb, a story, and a journey. And this brings us back to the deepest truths about reality and relationships.

TAKEAWAYS FROM CHAPTER EIGHTEEN

- A fifth characteristic of New Copernicans is their priority on relationships.
- The universe is a verb.
- Reality is relational and love is at the root of all reality.
- We need to recapture the Celtic practice of "belonging before believing."
- Nouning is a precursor to judging.

DISCUSSION QUESTIONS FOR CHAPTER EIGHTEEN

- How is social media technology a benefit to relationships?
- What is meant by reality being understood as a verb or a noun?
- What is the difference in seeing immigration as a verb or a noun? How might this change our attitude toward other hot-button issues?
- How are tattoos a way of seeing embodiment as a verb? Do you have any tattoos? What is the story behind them?

NINETEEN

AUTHENTICITY

COURT JESTERS

If you're familiar with the legend of King Arthur and his Round Table, you may have missed an important feature that should be taken into account. The Round Table consisted of the king, a wise sage (Merlin), a court jester (Dagonet), and the noble knights.[1] In Tennyson's epic poem cycle *Idylls of the King*, court jester Dagonet is the only one of the court who could foresee the coming doom of the kingdom. His prophetic and truth-telling insights were invaluable. The court jester is missing from most leadership roundtables and church leadership boards—the person who, with humor, can counter the natural tendency and danger of surrounding oneself with like-minded people. We, too, need to build conscious contrarian voices[2] into our leadership teams, and New Copernicans can provide that valuable corrective. We need people around us to expose our pretense, self-importance, and inauthenticity.

Millennials, if appropriately empowered, can provide the role of crap detector. This is because one of their highest ideals is authenticity. They don't put up with the fake, the superficial, or posers. They have a finely honed nose for pretense.

Authenticity is not a description that you can use for yourself; it is an affirmation given by others. It is a composite assessment of all a person is and does: "Are you being true to yourself? Are you being who you say you are to others?"[3] Only when there is integrity within the New Copernican frame—an integrity that is unforced, agenda free, and relationally saturated—will one approach the potential of authenticity. This is the gold-star aspiration of all who would connect with New Copernicans. It is not a pose one assumes, but a gift one receives.

James Gilmore and Joseph Pine have provided an entire book-length study on the importance of authenticity for business. Authenticity is important because fake products and services surround us—a condition social scientists describe as hyperreality. To encourage you to get an annual checkup from a real doctor, Cigna brought together an all-star team of fake doctors. We've got Alan Alda (*MASH*'s Franklin "Hawkeye" Pierce), Patrick Dempsey (Derek "McDreamy" Shepherd of *Grey's Anatomy*), Donald Faison (*Scrubs*' Christopher Turk), Noah Wyle (*ER*'s John Carter), and Lisa Edelstein (*House*'s Lisa Cuddy). The ad ends with the actors calling for a "doctor's pose." The ad is a spoof on a reality we have come to accept.

Western society, French sociologist and philosopher Jean Baudrillard claims, has undergone a "precession of simulacra."[4] In postmodern society the copies we make of reality have come to replace reality itself. Then we treat the copy as the reality. The process goes like this: (1) An image is a *reflection* of a basic reality; (2) The image *masks and perverts* the basic reality; (3) It *masks the absence* of a basic reality; and (4) This new hyperreality comes to *replace* the basic reality. The sign then becomes a simulacrum of the symbol. There is no *there* there, apart from the artificial world we have made. Artificiality replaces reality. The simulacrum becomes its own new reality, divorced from its original reference. This phenomenon is all around us, from drone strikes, to plastic surgery, to Wall Street trading. Let me illustrate the process.[5]

When making a film about the Alamo, the filmmakers deemed that the historic site was too small and unimposing. It lacked cinematic scale. So a new, larger replica was made outside of San Antonio. "Alamo Village had been a popular stop for Alamo fans for years. To many, it was more 'real' than the actual site," said Bruce Winders, Alamo historian.[6] It was closed indefinitely in 2010.

Architecture critic Ada Louise Huxtable has suggested that Americans prefer a good fake to a bad real, a slick lip-synch to strained vocals, a nip and tuck to natural imperfections. Illusion and reality are losing their distinctiveness.[7] Nowhere is this blurring more pronounced or accepted than in Las Vegas—the epicenter of this cultural phenomenon, the capital of Simulacra. Orlando's Walt Disney World runs a close second—where its "historic downtown" is only an architectural re-creation of an imagined faked past paved in cobblestones and lit with gaslights. Baudrillard claims, "Illusion is no longer possible, because the real is no longer possible."[8] What happens in Las Vegas stays in Las Vegas, because what happens is not really real. This is no longer marginal behavior reflective of exotic locations. Dr. Michael Salzhauer, a renowned plastic surgeon, wrote a children's book, *My Beautiful Mommy*, to help patients explain their surgical transformation to their children in a nonthreatening manner.

Business consultants Gilmore and Pine describe four modes of authenticity—real-real, real-fake, fake-real, and fake-fake. Authenticity is seen on a continuum based on answers to "Is it what it says it is?" and "Is it true to itself?"[9] In this kind of world, the millennial insistence on authenticity is a refreshing corrective. But it is also a sharp critique of evangelical experience and practice. A visit to any Christian bookstore will reveal that we are comfortable commercial purveyors of kitsch. On the Orlando Universal Studios tour, our guides told us, "The only thing real here is what you can see." We know that the gospel demands more than this. If we are living before an Audience of One, then our integrity must include the parts unseen, specifically our hearts. But if we are steeped in a culture of simulacra, where the fake is wink-wink accepted as real, then the importance and weight of this kind of integrity can diminish. Once again, we can be grateful for our millennial children who serve as our court jesters. We need their chastening, their blistering critique of the church. One of my sons left the church for a time out of disgust over the right-wing bumper stickers filling the church parking lot on Sunday morning. It appeared to him as if the gospel was being filtered through the lens of the Republican National Committee, rather than the gospel being the filter for politics and practice.[10] If we become defensive and don't listen, we will fail to appreciate their prophetic role in our lives.

The authentic presence of Christ is most often seen in the unscripted moments. A powerful example took place in 2013 in Saint Peter's Square when Pope Francis was speaking to a congregation of families. A little boy in a yellow shirt walked up to him on stage while he was speaking and hugged his leg and later crawled up on the pope's chair behind him.[11] The gentle acceptance and spontaneous love displayed in that unplanned moment meant more to that audience (and the audience watching worldwide) than any of his now-forgotten remarks. There is no substitute for authenticity. That millennials demand it, especially from people of faith, is a great and lasting benefit to the church. We must find ways to develop systems of reverse mentoring, empowering our fellow millennial New Copernican pilgrims to be court jesters, resident crap detectors in our midst. It is unlikely that we can see well enough without their assistance. Millennials are thus a valuable, nay, *essential* part of our church roundtable.

TAKEAWAYS FROM CHAPTER NINETEEN

- Missing from most leadership roundtables is a court jester.
- The sixth characteristic of New Copernicans is authenticity.
- It is difficult to be authentic without a court jester, a role that millennials are uniquely positioned to serve.
- New Copernicans do not put up with the fake, the superficial, or posers.
- Modern society greatly encourages the acceptance of the fake over the real.
- Authenticity is not a moniker you can take upon yourself, but is an affirmation gifted by others as evidence of one's public and private integrity.

DISCUSSION QUESTIONS FOR CHAPTER NINETEEN

- Why does the evangelical church desperately need court jesters?
- Do you consider the evangelical church to be real or authentic? Why or why not?
- Who is the most real person you have met? What were his or her characteristics?
- How is Christ seen in unscripted moments? Give examples.

TWENTY

HAUNTED

STANDING AT THE BROTHEL DOOR

Scottish writer Bruce Marshall, in his 1945 novel *The World, the Flesh, and Father Smith,* tells the story of Father Smith walking home one day when he encounters a beautiful, seductive young woman, Miss Dana Agdala. Aiming for a shock of sensibilities she introduces herself to Father Smith as the author of the scintillating and bestselling book, *Naked and Unashamed.* "But perhaps you haven't read me," she confesses.

She is a thoroughgoing modern. She asks the priest, "Tell me, do you get much response to the old, old story these days?" She had long ago rejected "all that poppycock about baptism, and purity, and the Virgin Birth" because, of course, "it's against all modern science and obstetrics." Like many people in her position, she had a lot of questions but had not had the chance to ask them of a Catholic priest.

Father Smith invited her to walk with him to his next

appointment. Among the many questions about the silliness of faith, she asks about his celibate sexuality. As she put it, "How do you manage to live without us?"

Easily and confidently, Father Smith answers that, in his view, "women's bodies are rarely perfect; they soon grow old and sag, and always the contemplation of them even at their best is a poor and boring substitute for walking with God in His House as a friend." Miss Agdala judges that Father Smith's answer proves what she had always maintained about Christians, "that religion is only a substitute for sex." Father Smith counters roundly, "I still prefer to believe that sex is a substitute for religion and that the young man who rings the bell at the brothel is unconsciously looking for God."[1]

This quote, often misappropriated to G. K. Chesterton, gets at a weakness of the church to appreciate the purpose and purity of desire. Too often we have been told in Christian homes, "Your desires (especially your sexual desires) are bad, and they will only get you in trouble. So you need to repress, ignore, or otherwise annihilate them. But follow all of these rules and you'll be a good, upstanding Christian citizen."[2] This is not Christianity, but stoicism. We do not need to reduce desire but increase it, and aim it at what we are really looking for. As C. S. Lewis is often quoted,

> If we consider the unblushing promises of reward and the staggering nature of the rewards promised in the Gospels, it would seem that our Lord finds our desires not too strong, but too weak. We are half-hearted creatures, fooling about with drink and sex and ambition when infinite joy is offered us, like an ignorant child who wants to go on making mud pies in a slum because he cannot imagine what is meant by the offer of a holiday at the sea. We are far too easily pleased.[3]

We need a renewed focus on desire and an appreciation for longing if we are to have an accurate assessment of human nature and a truly biblical anthropology. Philosopher James K. A. Smith argues, "Our primordial orientation to the world is not knowledge, or even belief, but *love*."[4] We are lovers and desirers before we are thinkers and analysts. If this is the case, then we will need to completely rethink our approach to apologetics. Can we set aside our apologetics based on worldviews and instead develop an apologetic based on desire? Smith continues, "What we love is a specific vision of the good life, an implicit picture of what we think human flourishing looks like. . . . A vision of the good life captures our hearts and imaginations not by providing a set of rules or ideas, but by painting a picture of what it looks like for us to flourish and live well."[5] Our lives are shaped first by our senses, second our imaginations, and then lastly by our intellects, a truth seen in the social imaginary of New Copernicans and their emphasis on living and learning through experience. In understanding them and this new social imaginary, it will be necessary to take their desires and longings seriously—these are the self-evident on-ramps for collaborative spiritual pilgrimage.

New Copernicans express their longings and desires both positively and negatively. Positively, they are seen in their desire to shape their lives and careers around "making the world a better place." Their social imaginary is filled with hopeful idealism. A reader commented in *The Seattle Times,* "For anyone who thinks that millennials are lazy, technology-obsessed, narcissistic zombies, I encourage you to look at the many millennials who are social workers, activists, writers, poets, artists, doctors, teachers and journalists—all of whom are doing what we believe in because we want to help make the world a better place."[6] This idealism is rooted in wanting to align one's life with a meaning and story larger than oneself and in promoting businesses with a triple bottom line (people, planet, and profits). For New Copernicans this is the positive functional equivalent of a religious quest.

These same aspirations put negatively are seen in their sense of haunting, their fear of missing out (FOMO). This is what secularity$_3$ feels like from the inside: a nagging fear that there is a story, meaning, or spiritual world larger than oneself that is the final validation of one's own personal plot. In this sense New Copernicans are like the ancient Celts, who were acutely aware of living in an enchanted world. Professor Tracy Balzer writes, "The earliest pagan Celts were profoundly aware of the spiritual world. Even before they came to know the one true God of the universe, they had an understanding of the unseen world, and perceived the reality of the spiritual world at every turn."[7] In this pagan, pantheistic spirituality, they believed there were places in nature where the line between the spirit world and the physical world was "tissue-paper thin." These revered liminal or threshold sacred sites became known as "thin places." And so it is true today that for many millennials, shared ecological concern and climate change are natural on-ramps for spiritual seeking. Nature is a means to God, a thin place—but not God. Their sensibility is not wrong as much as incomplete. The point of their spiritual pilgrimage is not the window, but what the window reveals beyond itself. Nature is not the place, but the portal.

This New Copernican sense of haunting generally falls into four portals or metanarratives: social justice, beauty or art, love or relationships, and spirit or spirituality. To these four, one could add suffering, but most New Copernicans are not old enough to have experienced the full weight of what life has in store for them. Jesus promises us that the foundations of every life will be eventually tested (Matt. 7:24–27). Every person will have a natural affinity to one or more of these portals. Theologian N. T. Wright describes these as "echoes of a voice: the longing for justice, the quest for spirituality, the hunger for relationships, and the delight in beauty."[8] These points of longing are valuable on-ramps for spiritual conversation and further progress on one's spiritual pilgrimage. For as Lewis observed, "Most people, if they had really learned to look into their hearts, would know that they do want, and want acutely, something that cannot be had in this world."[9] These longings are portals to a new spiritual journey toward a deeper reality.

The mission of the fellow pilgrim in the lives of these haunted New Copernicans is to affirm their longings and to point them to a relationship that adds to and completes these longings. If you are subtracting when you should be adding, you will always get the sum wrong. Too often the church is subtracting when it should be adding. We lament disenchantment—that the social world has less sensitivity to spiritual reality—when we should embrace the emerging spirit of reenchantment. We need less lament over what is not there and more seeking additional supernatural experience of what could be there. We should be celebrating that magic is once again in the air.

For we have the key that fits the lock of the deepest longings of the human heart. This was Tolkien and Dyson's message to C. S. Lewis on Addison's Walk after a dinner spent talking about metaphor and myth. Christianity is the answer to a real existential longing. Its interpretive power is not found in a philosophical argument so much as in the living of life and particularly living in the midst of one's deepest longings. This was the approach Francis Schaeffer took with nonbelievers: "Schaeffer believed the proper starting point in apologetics is not an authoritative insistence on the inerrancy of Scripture and the unverifiable truth of the Christian system but rather an appeal to the external world and internal states common in all humanity."[10] These longings are pointers to another world, to a larger story, to the myth that really happened. To effectively reach New Copernicans, we need to revive Lewis's argument from desire, the apologetics of the imagination and heart. The openness and FOMO longing of New Copernicans provide a ready point of contact, an on-ramp for spiritual pilgrimage. Burson and Walls summarize, "If our deepest longing is really for God, then that longing is a desire for heaven. At the heart of our apologetic task is the charge of helping people name their deepest longings."[11] It is for this reason that the door of the brothel, or the entrance of Burning Man's Orgy Dome, can be the threshold to a deeper pilgrimage. Their spiritual void leads them there and many will leave further dissatisfied with their regular lives as they continue to search for something more real. When the dust settles on Burning Man, many will face a deeper emptiness.

This is pretty much Father Smith's conclusion as well. In the end, what unites us is our shared longings and brokenness. Those pilgrims who are aware of both are the kind of people Jesus hangs with . . . then as well as now.

TAKEAWAYS FROM CHAPTER TWENTY

- The church frequently dismisses the purpose and purity of desire.
- We do not need to reduce desire, but increase it and aim it at what we are really looking for.
- Our basic orientation to the world is not knowledge but

love. We are lovers and desirers before we are thinkers and analysts.

- The church needs an apologetic based on desire.
- Desire and longing are self-evident on-ramps for collaborative spiritual pilgrimage.
- New Copernicans express their longings both positively and negatively: idealism and hauntedness.
- New Copernican longing and hauntedness falls into four narratives: social justice, beauty or art, love or relationships, and spirit or spirituality.
- The mission of fellow pilgrims is to affirm these longings and point them to a relationship that adds to and completes these longings.
- Christianity is the answer to a real existential longing.

DISCUSSION QUESTIONS FOR CHAPTER TWENTY

- Why is the church tone-deaf to desire? How does this reflect a wrong anthropology?
- How is this sense of hauntedness an on-ramp for spiritual conversation?
- Of the four kinds of hauntedness, which one do you have the most affinity for? How would you use it as a point of contact with a New Copernican?

PART FIVE

SURVIVAL STRATEGIES

We can collide with icebergs or navigate around them. Their presence in the water does not assume a direct confrontation or crash. With a careful watch set and a willingness to listen to our New Copernican navigators, we will learn a new way to steer in the coming frame shift. Once collision with the frame shift is averted, the real work—joining in authentic pilgrimage within the new frame—begins.

The spiritual pilgrimages of New Copernicans will all be different. When we are dealing with a person's hopes and dreams, aspirations and longings, we are on sacred soil. There are four common groupings of these longings, which provide on-ramps for joint exploration. These are survival strategies if the evangelical church is to join in their pilgrimages.

TWENTY-ONE

JUSTICE

I HAVE A DREAM

According to *Inc.* magazine, there is one question that most motivates millennials: "What is your dream?" Ask and listen.

In analyzing what motivates millennials in the workplace, reporter Emily Marks explains, "Motivational quotes on the wall don't build culture. Office trips to the bowling alley don't build culture. Drinks with the team or Monday morning donuts don't build culture. Those things create the *opportunity* for culture to be built—and real culture is formed through the understanding of one another. We are all human. We all have our own dreams, aspirations, hopes and ambitions."[1] Relationships trump motivational quotes.

It is in listening, encouraging, and equipping others in their dreams that deep human connection can transpire. The four on-ramps from New Copernican hauntedness to collaborative spiritual pilgrimage are justice, beauty, love, and spirit. Their level of intensity with each on-ramp will differ for every person, and some will have strong feelings about more than one. It is also true that there may be more than these four on-ramps. But what we can say is that here one must walk gently, for we are on relational sacred ground. There is no room for manipulation or hidden agendas. These are not on-ramps for evangelism, but on-ramps for human connection.

Since the evangelical church could do better in cultivating agenda-free, noninstrumental relationships, we'll look at each of these four over the course of the next four chapters. When we are dealing with something that is so precious to another person, their hopes and dreams, their aspirations and longings, there are both opportunities and dangers.

Perhaps the culturally safest and most common of these four longings is discussions about social justice. Generally, this is the backdrop to New Copernicans' desire to "make the world a better place." Whether it is with people, animals, or nature, the underlying desire is to put things to right. It is recognition of what is: that the world is not what it ought to be, and that something can be done about it. No one denies the four notes of justice: *ought, is, can,* and *will be.*[2] New Copernicans don't find it as important to have adequate epistemological or metaphysical grounding for their ethical aspirations—the kind of questions that arise from a scorched earth, overly intellectualized apologetic approach. Instead, it is enough to have a sense of moral outrage in a particular area of life. Their comfort is with the lived experience, not the cognitive abstraction.

This outrage can take many different expressions, from climate change to police brutality to animal rights to racism to LGBTQ rights to immigrants to human trafficking to bullying. Among the social justice community there is usually a shared portfolio of outrage.

The church needs to avoid several mistakes here. First, do not primarily see these concerns as political. If a person has sufficient outrage about a particular area of life, it is always personal before it is political. What is important is how your outrage connects with *your* story. If your first impulse is to see an issue in political terms— Democrat, Republican, Independent, Libertarian, or Socialist—you will have completely missed the point and not see the longing as a part of the person's story or, dare I add, identity. What is interesting is the personal pain, not the public policy. Avoid framing these longings as political science abstractions rather than as existential relational identity markers. In some circles there is criticism about identity politics. For New Copernicans it is always identity politics.

We'd do well to avoid Hillary Clinton's mistake when she engaged Black Lives Matter activists in Keene, New Hampshire. Fueled by social media, outrage over police brutality targeting black men, and a shared experience of protest, this social movement has a democratic and relationally driven leadership structure consisting of an ad hoc policy platform that brings together young people with a wide assortment of priorities and agendas. When they interrupted her campaign stop, Clinton asked them for policy recommendations, but she asked the wrong question, just as we are most prone to do. Arguing that the movement can't change deep-seated racism, Clinton said,

> Look, I don't believe you change hearts. I believe you change laws, you change allocation of resources, you change the way systems operate. You're not going to change every heart. You're not. But at the end of the day, we could do a whole lot to change some hearts and change some systems and create more opportunities for people who deserve to have them, to live up to their own God-given potential.[3]

She gave a left-brain answer to a right-brain question. A better response by Clinton would have been, "When can I join you in your next protest?" Solidarity is not affirmed by principle or policy but via a shared experience. The church will need to participate in the meaningful experiences of others, rather than creating our own experiences for them to join. Certainly this is riskier, but it is also far more relationally connected. We need to set foot on their turf, not merely invite them to ours. The opportunity is to engage in people's dreams of a better world, to share in the personal pain that has led to public protest—not an opportunity to argue about public policy or theological doctrine. It is an opportunity to see life through relational eyes. Our task in these encounters is listening, empathy, and participation. It is learning to walk in another person's shoes at least for a moment on their path. Connection, conversation, and compassion: this is the opportunity that these on-ramps afford.

New Copernicans will have no interest in God's love for them if we don't show sacrificial care first, particularly in the arena of their greatest passion and outrage. We don't have to agree with another person's politics or protest tactics to understand the universal general rightness of moral outrage and its inevitable close association with their woundedness. We must approach these on-ramps through a personal rather than a political frame. The unity is in the longing, a longing that can be affirmed and embraced.

We see this pattern in Jesus: seeing, caring, acting. We need to see before we act. It is said of Jesus, "When he *saw* the crowds, he had *compassion* on them" (Matt. 9:36, emphasis added). Too often we look away, feign ignorance, to avoid moral culpability. Like the priest and Levite in the story of the Good Samaritan, we tend to "pass by on the other side" of the road. Isn't this the way we typically handle panhandlers when we're in our cars? When they come up to our car window at the intersection, we look away and start fiddling with the radio.

I've made it a spiritual discipline to always look and to always give something. I even gave to the homeless man who had a sign that read, "Need money for beer." I do it for *me* as much as for the other person, so that I don't become the kind of person who looks away from the world as it ought not to be. And I was feeling pretty self-righteously good about this practice until one day I was taught a deeper lesson.

I was sitting in Starbucks in Boston next to the Commons, when a homeless woman entered and began asking all the patrons for money one at a time. I was ready. When she came to me, I looked in her eyes and gave her a few dollars and then went about what I was doing. A few minutes later she came back to my table and said, "And by the way, my name is Sarah." Her point: genuine compassion involves investing in the personal. Put differently, she said to me, "Friend, Jesus would have done more. He would have seen me as a person with a name first, and not a project or spiritual discipline. My name is Sarah." I still give money, but I now ask their name.

It was when Doral Chenoweth, a videographer for the *Columbus Dispatch*, stopped to ask Ted Williams his name that this homeless radio host and voice-over artist was saved.[4] The social justice outrage of New Copernicans, their dreams of making the world a better place, starts by asking their names, exploring their dreams by listening, and participating in their journey of working for shalom.

TAKEAWAYS FROM CHAPTER TWENTY-ONE

- The question, "What is your dream?" is one of the most motivating questions to ask a millennial.

- The safest and most common longing among New Copernicans is social justice.
- The social justice longing touches on the four notes of the gospel: *ought*, *is*, *can*, and *will be*.
- There is in the social justice community a portfolio of moral outrage; the deepest issues are always tied to identity.
- To connect with a person's longing for social justice one needs to see, care, and collaborate.
- We must approach these on-ramps through a personal rather than a political frame.

DISCUSSION QUESTIONS FOR CHAPTER TWENTY-ONE

- What is the danger of politicizing a person's longing for social justice or outrage over social injustice?
- How can we cause greater problems by being too quick to give answers? What is most often needed instead of answers?
- How can we each become the kind of person who sees, cares, and collaborates?

TWENTY-TWO

BEAUTY

MUSIC SENT TO HEAVEN

In his classic Russian novel *The Brothers Karamazov*, Dostoyevsky observes "beauty is the battlefield where God and Satan contend with each other for the hearts of men."[1] Beauty is the doorway to the imagination and is thus closely related to our loves. It is not surprising that many of the storytelling cultural creatives that curate our national social imaginary—the stories we tell about the good life—are artists. One thinks of Tom Wolfe, Makoto Fujimura, Martin Scorsese, Mary McCleary, J. J. Abrams, Anne Lamott, David Oyelowo, and Jacob Marshall. These artists are often those who are most sensitive to the coming frame shift we've discussed. The church has much to learn from them, for their sensitivities are instructive, even prophetic. Since the Romantic movement, beauty has often been associated with spirituality. This connection is deeper and more enduring than many moderns realize.

The ancients spoke of a unified relationship between three

transcendental realities: truth, goodness, and beauty. If the political culture was concerned with goodness and the academic culture with truth, then the artistic culture was concerned with beauty. For the ancients, beauty was not just a subjective aspiration of an individual—as in "I just like it," merely a matter of personal taste—but the intuitive immediate awareness of a harmonious objective reality that points to something beyond itself. Beauty is goodness and truth expressed in an embodied transrational manner. When things are put right, one experiences beauty. Music professor Julian Johnson writes, "To an earlier age, our contemporary idea of a complete relativism in musical judgment would have seemed nonsensical. One could no more make valid individual judgments about musical values than about science. Music was no more 'a matter of taste' than was the orbit of the planets or the physiology of the human body. From Plato to Hemholtz, music was understood to be based on natural laws, and its value was derived from its capacity to frame and elaborate these laws in musical form."[2] It is for this reason that beauty does not call us inward to a therapeutic individualism, but outward to another world away, to a shared community of harmony and oughtness. Its important role in our worship is not surprising. Theologian N. T. Wright states, "Beauty points away from the present world to a different one altogether."[3]

It is not necessary for nonbelieving New Copernican artists to agree with this ancient assessment of art. However, this ancient understanding provides a rationale for the pull of beauty. When a character in Dostoyevsky's novel *The Idiot* says, "Beauty will save the world," he is recognizing that beauty compels us in ways that we cannot always understand or appreciate.[4] It calls us to our truest self and to an accurate assessment of reality.

After years of ignoring artists, many churches have established ministries to them. Many times we are trying to reach artists in very unartistic ways. Left-brained preaching is rarely effective in reaching these connoisseurs of a right-brained perspective. Moreover, artists are not simply a target audience for church membership, but the church's master mentors—both nonbelieving and believing artists—that we need in developing spirituality aligned with the New Copernican frame shift. The evangelical church needs artists and the artists' sensibility a lot more than artists need the church.

Consider music. Music is sound organized by rhythm (the tempo in time), melody (the linear arrangement of tones), harmony (the simultaneous sounding of different tones), texture (the effect of the composite arrangement of tempo and tones), and structure (the design of the piece as a whole). Music is vibrations arranged in time in order to express meaning and beauty, which connects with the human imagination and points to its transcendent origin. Because music is physical in nature, one's view of music is necessarily a reflection of one's view of reality—the true, good, and beautiful. Austrian literary critic Leo Spitzer, in his book *Classical and Christian Ideas of World Harmony*, argues that music is a metaphor of the cosmos.[5] A musical score reveals a composer's metaphysical perspective. Jazz great John Coltrane said, "Overall, I think the main thing a musician would like to do is to give a picture to the listener of the many wonderful things he knows and senses in the universe. That's what music is to me—it's just another way of saying this is a big, beautiful universe we live in, that's been given to us, and here's an example of just how magnificent and encompassing it is. That's what I would like to do. I think that's one of the greatest things you can do in life, and we all try to do in some way."[6] And when it is done well, it is a gift to all.

Artists of all stripes—painters, sculptors, musicians, dancers, photographers, fashion designers, theatrical artists, and filmmakers—have three things to give us, if we listen well to their longings. They bring us in contact with beauty, they celebrate the value of creativity, and they strengthen our appreciation of intuition and the right hemisphere of the brain. These are all weaknesses in the current evangelical church and are each a call to a more balanced and humane faith expression and understanding of reality. With the New Copernican shift, the day of the artist has come. New Copernican artists are the church's master mentors—if she is humble to listen to them.

For too long artists have felt alienated from the church, unappreciated at many levels. When the evangelical church embraced them, it was often for their propagandistic value—to communicate an evangelistic message or churchy preaching.[7] This is a left-brain distortion of a right-brain gift. We have thereby turned artists into something other than artists, violated the terms of their art, and discounted the unique aspirations of their longing. To appreciate artists' longing for beauty, we will need to honor their frame, respect their intuition, and give them a voice.

Art is not value-neutral. It always embodies a view of reality. And even when we might disagree with this view, a particular artistic worldview, we can affirm the value of their longing and the intuitive sensibilities that this longing reveals. If the evangelical church is to gain more balance, we'll need a much larger dose of this sensibility than we have presently allowed. If beauty will save the world, we'd best start with the evangelical church.

My father was a missionary cancer surgeon. He had the heart

of an artist expressed as a gifted violinist. It was not surprising that his favorite poem was English Victorian poet Robert Browning's "Abt Vogler."

> All we have willed or hoped or dreamed of good shall exist;
> Not its semblance, but itself; no beauty, nor good, nor power
> Whose voice has gone forth, but each survives for the melodist
> When eternity affirms the conception of an hour.
> The high that proved too high, the heroic for earth too hard,
> The passion that left the ground to lose itself in the sky;
> Are music sent up to heaven by the lover and the bard;
> Enough that he heard it once: we shall hear it by and by.[8]

Beauty for this "earth too hard" will be sent to heaven and be heard by and by. Beauty is a call to another world away. We are most fortunate when given the opportunity of awe and wonder to enter into this experience. There are many with whom we can join on their aesthetic spiritual pilgrimage. We turn now to the universal longing for love.

TAKEAWAYS FROM CHAPTER TWENTY-TWO

- Many of the most influential storytelling cultural creatives who curate the public social imaginary are artists.
- Beauty is the second on-ramp for spiritual pilgrimage.
- Beauty calls us to recognize a transcendent reality.
- The evangelical church needs artists and the artists' sensibility a lot more than artists need the church.

DISCUSSION QUESTIONS FOR CHAPTER TWENTY-TWO

- How can we develop our artistic sensibilities?
- How can we treat artists in an artistic manner?
- How does our church honor or support artists?
- How have we reached out to artists within our local community?

TWENTY-THREE

LOVE

THE UNIVERSAL LONGING

Many in the church cannot hear the cultural longing for love. A Puritanical moralism blocks our ability to enter into this widespread and controversial longing. Because it gets mixed up with sex and marriage, we cannot affirm the validity of this longing as longing. Love is not only about sex and marriage; one thinks of love of neighbor. However, one must not diminish the compelling power and purpose of eros. Sex and love are intended to be seen as one and not pitted against each other. James K. A. Smith, on his reading of Augustine, makes no distinction between love and desire: "*Agape* is rightly directed eros."[1]

This longing and desire is compounded and compelled by loneliness. In a hyperconnected world, our sense of loneliness is placed on steroids. Mother Teresa observes, "The greatest disease in the West today is not TB or leprosy; it is being unwanted, unloved, and uncared for. We can cure physical diseases with medicine, but the only cure for loneliness, despair, and hopelessness is love. There are many in the world who are dying for a piece of bread but there are many more dying for a little love."[2] It has been estimated that approximately sixty million people in the United States, or 20 percent of the total population, feel lonely.[3]

Somehow the church cannot validate the secular language of love if it is set in the hookup culture of college campuses, an LGBTQ pride parade, or a crowded bar late on a Friday night. Yet these are the settings where this longing finds its strongest expression. Loneliness is a powerful and crippling emotion, and it can't be solved alone. By its very definition it demands the other, or better the Other.

The church gets this need for love and belonging, but as soon as sex is involved, we have a severe empathy cramp. We somehow cannot look past the sex to the loneliness, past the questioned behavior to the overwhelming desire to love and be loved. If we would listen, we'd find that sex is an epicenter in the longing for love. It was designed to be that way.

In relationships today sex means very little; however, verbally affirming one's love for another is a big deal. This phenomenon is seen each season on the reality TV show *The Bachelor* and *The Bachelorette*. Many contestants have been rejected simply because they have not crossed this enormous hurdle soon enough. The L-word is everything.

The same thing is true of LGBTQ relationships. Regardless of one's political or theological views, and particularly so, "love wins" is a true statement. The root of everyone's longing is to be loved.

Christopher West, the Catholic popularizer of Pope John Paul II's Theology of the Body, describes the arch of our universal longing in terms of desire, design, and destiny. Philosopher Peter Kreeft argues that human sexuality is derived from cosmic sexuality, that we are a specific example of a universal principle. Kreeft writes, "We fit; we are not freaks. What we are, everything else is also, though in different ways and different degrees. We are, to use the medieval image, a microcosm, a little cosmos; the universe is the macrocosm, the same pattern written large. . . . [And this] means that sexuality goes all the way up and all the way down the cosmic ladder."[4] His point is that human sexuality is not merely a human or social construct, but grounded in the very nature of reality. Our bodies have a design and purpose. Our sexuality is designed to call us into an intimate relationship with God, to make visible an invisible reality. This is Paul's message in Ephesians, "For this reason a man will leave his father and mother and be united to his wife, and the two will become one flesh. *This is a profound mystery—but I am talking about Christ and the church*" (Eph. 5:31–32, emphasis added). In short, God wants to marry us. Christopher West expands, "God is infinitely *other*, infinitely *different* from his creation. And yet this infinitely different Creator does not hold himself aloof. God wants to be *one* with his creation. God wants to *unite* with his creation. God wants to *marry* his creation. This is what the mystery of Jesus Christ—the mystery of God taking on flesh—is all about: the marriage of Creator and creature; the marriage of divinity and humanity."[5]

And so it should not be surprising that if love is the root of all reality and that God's primary purpose is to marry us, that love should be such a strong longing and most susceptible for distortion and confusion. The Latin phrase *corruptio optimi pessima est* ("the corruption of the best things are the worst things") makes sexuality a likely subject of reality's brokenness.

But the question we must ask ourselves is, do we have to get to design or specific sexual morality to honor desire? And the answer is clearly no. Using the universal longings for love as a springboard spiritual conversation is enough. One does not need to immediately affirm any particular sexual ethic. This is seen routinely at Oriented to Love retreats.

Evangelicals for Social Action's Oriented to Love dialogues help Christ followers come together around the highly charged and challenging topic of sexual and gender diversity in the church. The goal is to find unity that is deeper than agreement. How can Christians love each other across sharp disagreements about what faithful sexuality looks like? How can we listen respectfully in order to truly see and know those we disagree with rather than vilify and dismiss each other?[6]

At these retreats it is demonstrated again and again that the unifying love of Jesus can and does supersede theological and personal differences on gender and sexuality. We do well to keep first things the first things, to affirm the validity of the longing for love as the on-ramp to spiritual exploration.

What we will find is that we don't have to say everything or agree on anything to be loving. As we enter into the spiritual pilgrimages of others, we don't have to have the posture of knowing all the answers; we can genuinely listen to their stories and learn from their own search for meaning, we can express our failures and weaknesses, and at the same time we can rely on and expect the presence of Christ to be the silent partner in our shared journey. More important than our persuasive ability is the authenticity of our presence and our daily reliance on Christ in all things, which enables us to channel the reality of Christ to others.

From our perspective it may seem that we are simply muddling through together on this joint pilgrimage. It may sometimes seem like the blind leading the blind. But this is not so. Guardrails are often added to the most dangerous sections of a hiking trail. The guardrails on both sides of the path help one move forward safely. God does the same for novice spiritual pilgrims with two sets of guardrails: the Holy Spirit within and lived experience without.

Internally, the Holy Spirit is invisibly working in all the lives we encounter. He is the one who knows best how to address heart issues. We do not need to, nor should we want to, take the place of the Holy Spirit. He is the one who will finally guide us home. Our confidence in his presence means that we can abandon all forms of coercion. God is the Good Shepherd, and he is in the business of finding lost sheep. He is the active agent in our collective sacred journeys. The circumstances of our pilgrimage, even the shape and depth of our heart's longings, are finally under the dictates of his loving providence.

The other guardrail is reality itself. If reality has a design—because it's made by a Creator—then engaging reality in life will guide us by trial and error to what serves human flourishing and what does not. In discussing her film *Friends with Benefits*, actress Mila Kunis notes honestly, "Having friends with benefits is a lot like communism. It works well in theory, but not so well in execution."[7] The more we resist the dictates of reality, the more tension we will feel in life, a kind of ontological dissonance. The existential rub is not in the argument but in the living.[8] Before moral debates about sexuality, we need to ask the bigger framing question: What is the purpose of sexuality? What is the purpose of my body? Theological and ethical arguments over sexuality rarely move or influence a person. Learning the contours of love from the reality of relationships with their longings and loss is a far better teacher. Many pastors may be hesitant to be quite so open-ended about sexuality, but in a been-there-done-that world where people are working off of antithetical frames from the Bible, I'm not sure that there is much of an alternative. Here experience may have to be the default teacher, however costly.

While the dictates of reality can be resisted—one can still fall over the cliff—those who are genuine seekers are in a better position to learn from them. God's claim is that "you will . . . find me when you seek me with all your heart" (Jer. 29:13). This is why we must celebrate all who are seeking, all who are muddling through their honest pilgrimage. There is no human thriving without being on a spiritual journey. And the first discussion on this journey need not be one about our differences in sexual ethics. If it is, then it only goes to show our own degree of sexual hang-ups. For just as the human reality of the alien takes precedence over immigration public policy discussions, so, too, do the longings for love. These longings, and the loneliness that often precedes them, are in themselves sacred portals to transcendence. There is a groom here waiting for his bride. It is enough to embrace the longing, for here we help point seekers to Christ. The New Copernican intuits that sex is about something more than sex, a call to the deeper spiritual reality of love.

TAKEAWAYS FROM CHAPTER TWENTY-THREE

- Our Puritanical moralism tends to block our ability to enter into the cultural longing for love.
- Twenty percent of the American population is struggling with loneliness.
- As soon as sex is involved, people in the church get an empathy cramp.

- The longing for love is among the strongest and most important relational longings, one that exceeds sex but includes it.
- We must be able to talk about the desire for love apart from further discussions about its design and destiny.
- We don't have to say everything or agree on anything to be loving.
- There are internal and external guardrails to guide us on our mutual pilgrimage of seeking love: the Holy Spirit within and reality without.
- All genuine seekers find.

DISCUSSION QUESTIONS FOR CHAPTER TWENTY-THREE

- What are the internal and external guardrails that guide our experience and conversations about love?
- Which of the two guardrails do you have the hardest time believing is at work to guide seekers?
- How can we affirm the unity of longing without getting sucked into debates about sexual ethics or theological disagreements?
- Why must we celebrate all who are genuinely seeking?

TWENTY-FOUR

SPIRIT

PILGRIMAGE OF THE HEART

New Copernicans have an innate restlessness stemming from an acute awareness of an existential disconnect between what is and what ought to be. The hauntedness for transcendence seen in them creates an opportunity for the church. This hauntedness reflects the personality and experiences of each person. Few see the connection between their passion for justice, appreciation of beauty, and longing for love as a desire for God. Few will make the spiritual connection. However, most would be aware that it is important to them to enfold their own story into a larger frame of meaning, even if it is the clichéd aspiration of "making the world a better place."

However, there are some who take this restlessness into the spiritual realm. And when they do it is typically not to traditional institutional religious expressions. They live in a been-there-done-that world, and in most cases the Christian church is written off as a spiritual cul-de-sac. It is not that they are so against the church—unless they have had bad experiences with it in their past—but that they see no real potential value there. Many are more put off by the church's 2-D framing of reality associated with a closed transcendent perspective than they are with Christian faith itself. They disavow the Enlightenment framing of faith and so look to 3-D religious expressions.[1]

Nor are they looking for a more hip and relevant church. There certainly are these kinds of hip churches that are reaching millennials. Laura DaSilva reflects on Toronto's C3 church. She writes, "With an avant-garde rock band, an Australian pastor in skinny jeans at the mic and Drake-inspired graphics behind him, C3 might seem more like Coachella than what it really is—church."[2] While it might seem that C3 is countering the point being made here, behind the superficiality of its self-evident hipness, members at C3 acknowledge that what they really seek is meaning, acceptance, and community. What is also true is that C3 is a Pentecostal church, where the immediacy of spiritual reality, the power of the Holy Spirit, and tangibility of God's real presence is embraced. This is a church that accepts the notion of sacramental thin places.

What is more important than style points—cooler bands, hipper worship, edgier programming, and audiovisual technology—is a desire for unvarnished spiritual reality. Rachel Held Evans warns, "Young people don't simply want a better show. And trying to be cool might make things worse."[3] She has statistics to prove her point. She writes, "I'm not the only millennial whose faith couldn't be saved by lacquering on a hipper veneer. According to the Barna Group, among young people who don't go to church, 87% say they see Christians as judgmental, and 85% see them as hypocritical. A similar study found that 'only 8% say they don't attend because church is out of date.'"[4]

This raises the general question: How do churches effectively reach New Copernicans? My assessment is that churches need to provide authentic experiences of following Jesus into the arenas of their deepest longings (justice, beauty, love, and spirit), giving them an opportunity to connect their personal story with a larger narrative of meaning, particularly couched in a relationally humble 3-D posture. Millennials want to see that you practice what you preach, that you love the world you live in through your work and not just your words.

Most importantly, this will require revamping how we think about, frame, and teach evangelism. Even the word *evangelism* is a stumbling block for many millennials.[5] The immediate reaction is "What are you trying to sell me or do to me that I don't want?" This is a fair reaction in light of the church's typical approach. We need a new picture for evangelism. It is less about closing a mortgage as joining an exploration.

We can overcome this need to "do evangelism"—what is pejoratively perceived by the typical New Copernican as "doing proselytizing"—by picturing in our minds a shared pilgrimage rather than London's Hyde Park Speakers Corner. It is not that followers of Jesus have arrived and we are calling others to our settled destination—which is the typical closed transcendent framing of evangelism. That is *not* the picture to have if we are to be effective in connecting with the contemporary nonbeliever. We must hold in our minds the picture of joining together on a shared spiritual pilgrimage to a yet undeclared destination. It is less important that we are conceptually heading in the same direction or going the same speed, but that we are on a shared trail together and that our paths have for this moment meaningfully crossed. What is important is to make this path crossing, however long or short, deeply meaningful, genuinely human, aesthetically beautiful, and hopefully memorable. It is in this shared relational experience of spiritual companionship on an open-ended spiritual adventure that God works in the pilgrim's life. We will also be changed for the better in the process. Rabbi Abraham Joshua Heschel put it best, "Faith is not the clinging to a shrine, but an endless pilgrimage of the heart."[6]

What is the role of the Bible in these shared pilgrimages? Its role is significant, but in a manner that is markedly different from the way it has been used in the past. The emphasis needs to be on the story of the Bible, rather than on the Bible as a book. We must learn to picture the narrative arc of the Bible in a manner that captures the imagination, rather than using the Bible as a source of modernistic proof texts. We must learn to embed our lives within the larger biblical drama. Bartholomew and Goheen do this in their book, *The Drama of Scripture: Finding Our Place in the Biblical Story*. They write, "Are we left with our own personal stories to make sense of our lives? Or is there a true story that is bigger than both of us, through which we can understand the world and find meaning for our lives? Are our personal stories—apart and together—parts of a more comprehensive story?"[7] Modern Bible readers tend to see things in fragments, memorize favorite verses, and thereby lose a sense of the whole, the Bible's narrative arc. New Zealand theologian David Williams writes,

> Before the Bible is anything else, it is story. The dynamic tension and drama and adventure of that story need to be recovered by storytellers for a generation that is hungry for stories. Culture has become immune to the drama of this particular story, perhaps because other forms of knowing have obscured its preposterous

character. If we don't tell the story well, we will not engage the culture in the way the story deserves and demands.[8]

There is a great deal of openness in the wider culture to the practice of mindfulness, a kind of secular meditative practice based loosely on Buddhism.[9] Though fundamentally different in its spiritual origins and orientation, one might rightly propose that reading the Bible meditatively is a portal to a wider spiritual reality. Bible reading is a thin place. Meditating quietly on Psalm 23 or Romans 8 has a way of allowing the Holy Spirit to work existentially in one's life in ways that are even beyond our conscious mind. Thirty consecutive days of thirty-minute meditative Scripture reading will change the reader and will appreciably enhance their awareness of a wider spiritual reality. This is not typically how the Bible has been brought into the discussion of evangelism. This is not the "Roman Road" of evangelism, but the Holy Spirit's open road.

New Copernicans desire and look for a personal encounter with spiritual reality. There is no conceivable reason why an ordinary apprentice of Jesus who is indwelt by the Holy Spirit can't become for that seeker a Wi-Fi hotspot for the kingdom of God.[10] The central message of Jesus is that the "kingdom of God has come near" (Mark 1:15). He meant by this that all around us is God's presence and power and that his spiritual presence and power is available to us as we acknowledge him in all that we do. Writer Madeleine L'Engle reminds us of the obvious: "We draw people to Christ not by loudly discrediting what they believe, by telling them how wrong they are and how right we are, but by showing them a light that is so lovely that they want with all their hearts to know the source of it."[11] By God's grace and because of our humble reliance on him, God's presence, God's love, God's forgiveness, and

God's reality should be evident in who we are, if we have entered into a personal relationship with Jesus and have apprenticed our lives to him. It is for this reason that our "being" is more important than our "talking." There is, finally, no substitute for the indwelling reality of a loving Christ seen in and through our lives. It is this presence that makes our encounters with others different. It is in this manner that the New Copernican longings can be on-ramps to spiritual exploration.

TAKEAWAYS FROM CHAPTER TWENTY-FOUR

- New Copernicans also take their haunted restlessness into the realm of the spirit and spirituality. However, typically it is not toward traditional institutional religious expressions.
- Most New Copernicans are more put off by the 2-D framing of reality associated with a closed transcendent perspective than they are with Christian faith itself. We have a framing problem as much as a faith problem.
- For churches to effectively reach New Copernicans, they need to provide authentic experiences of following Jesus into the arenas of their deepest longings, giving them an opportunity to connect their personal story with a larger narrative of meaning couched in a relationally humble 3-D posture.
- The Bible needs to be used in a manner that emphasizes story—its narrative arc—rather than the Bible as a book or merely a compilation of proof texts.
- An ordinary apprentice of Jesus who is indwelt by the Holy Spirit is a Wi-Fi hotspot for the kingdom of God for all he or she is in contact with.

DISCUSSION QUESTIONS FOR CHAPTER TWENTY-FOUR

- In some hip churches, it is more than their hipness that connects effectively with millennials. What are some of these other factors?
- Do you see those factors in your churches, or are there places that need to improve?
- Why is *evangelism* a problem term for New Copernicans? How can we correct this problem?
- What is the role of the Bible in these shared spiritual pilgrimages?

PART SIX

WHAT CRISIS LEADERSHIP DEMANDS

Millennials are familiar with the iceberg-strewn ocean of the coming frame shift. As such they are the best harbor pilots to navigate these waters. It is for this reason that millennial New Copernicans are the hope of the church. It is difficult for a parent to give the keys to the car to their teenage driver. It is equally difficult for a child to take away the keys from an aging parent. These kinds of transitions are difficult but often necessary. The transition of leadership to emerging millennial church leaders is vital for the evangelical church.

TWENTY-FIVE

CHANGING TRUMP CARDS

The late French social theorist Pierre Bourdieu compared a social community's engagement with the wider culture to playing a card game. Within each community there are certain rules, expectations, and dynamics required for success. Someone gifted in the game does not give these rules a second thought, as they are second nature to them, assumed as the subconscious backdrop to the game play. It is only when the game changes, say from Spades to Hearts, that the different nuances of the rules and game play become conscious once again. If the players do not adjust to the new game, they are certain to be left holding a losing hand.

These social rules of the game Bourdieu calls *habitus*. They are the historically derived dispositions of thought and practice, the deep unconscious assumptions about how one successfully navigates social life within a given field of social endeavor. He writes, "I am talking about dispositions acquired through experience, thus variable from place to place and time to time."[1] Or as he states elsewhere, these deep structures are a historically constituted, institutionally grounded—and thus a socially variable—generative matrix. A simple way of thinking about habitus is "history swallowed." A community's assumptions about life are shaped by attitudes and experiences derived over time. They weigh heavily on the individual and unconsciously influence the decisions an individual or institution will make. While they are not determinative, they are determining. There is weight to habitus.

This is true of all communities, but it is especially true of American evangelicals. It has long been noted by historians of evangelicalism that evangelicals do not generally operate with any consistency in public based on their theology. Rather their behavior is based on their habitus and in this case a selective appropriation of American history. Karl Marx observes, "Men make their own history, but they do not make it just as they please; they do not make it under circumstances chosen by themselves, but under circumstances directly encountered, given, and transmitted from the past."[2] Bourdieu adds, "It is yesterday's man who inevitably predominates us."[3]

American evangelical public engagement is shaped by five characteristics, each reflective of a particular period of American history. At least five can be identified: reign, revival, resentment, retreat, and reassertion. Here we will only give a brief overview of the evangelical habitus (for more information, see *The Evangelical Forfeit*[4]).

The first characteristic is *American exceptionalism*. American evangelical identity is closely tied to America's myth of origin. The picture is of a "city on a hill" and the historical source for this habitus is 1630–1800. The emphasis on a Christian America, framer's intent, and manifest destiny all find their sources in the nation's Puritan ethos. Though it is clearly a mixed bag, historian Sidney Ahlstrom concludes, "Puritanism provided the moral and religious background of fully 75 percent of the people who declared their independence in 1776."[5] Too often evangelicals confuse the flag with the cross. And yet we come by this confusion honestly, for the interdependence of Christian and American democracy is real. As early as 1835, Alexis de Tocqueville noted, "It must never be forgotten that religion gave birth to Anglo-American society. In the United States, religion is therefore mingled with all the habits of the nation and all the feelings of patriotism, whence it derives a particular force."[6] There is thus a very real sense that Christianity has a sense of reigning, a latent majoritarian impulse.

The second characteristic is *populism*, stemming from the revivals of the Second Great Awakening. The picture here is "We the people," and the time frame is 1800–1880. During this period frontier populism replaced East Coast Puritanism. Populism remains one of the deepest impulses of the evangelical habitus.[7] Historian Nathan Hatch writes, "The rise of evangelical Christianity in the early republic is, in some measure, a story of the success of common people in shaping the culture after their own priorities rather than the priorities outlined by gentlemen such as the framers of the Constitution."[8] This characteristic explains the tendency for anti-elitism, conspiracy theories, anti-intellectualism, grassroots advocacy, and nativism. In the nineteenth century social reform and evangelistic fervor were a unified mission. Hatch concludes that populism is the driving force in American evangelicalism.

The third characteristic is *resentment*, stemming from the loss of cultural dominance of the church between 1880–1930. It was during this fifty-year period that Protestant evangelical Christianity lost its cultural hegemony. There are multiple factors as to why this happened, including the rise of Darwin, Freud, and Nietzsche. The impact of biblical critical theory, Eastern European immigration, and urbanization also played a role. During the interwar years (1920–30) sociologists

Robert and Helen Lynd concluded in their famous Middletown study that during this period religion shifted from "a set of beliefs to a social occasion" (as in Easter and Christmas).[9] This period is highlighted by the infamous Scopes trial in 1925, which served as a kind of cultural Custer's Last Stand. The overwhelming sense from this period is that something precious has been lost.

The fourth characteristic was the *creation of an evangelical subculture*, a retreat from culture to subculture, from center to periphery, during the period stemming from 1930–70. It was during this period that most of the current evangelical institutions were formed, from *Christianity Today* to Fuller Theological Seminary. There was in this period a theological hardening with the rise of fundamentalism and a decided self-marginalization culturally symbolized by *Christianity Today*'s move from Washington to Wheaton. Evangelicalism moved from being a dominant cultural player to being a peripheral niche market. This subcultural mindset continues today in faith-based films that are scripted to preach to the converted.[10]

Finally, beginning in the 1970s we see an *evangelical cultural reassertion*, initially to the privatized domain of family and home. Sociologist James Davison Hunter writes,

> Protestants long ago conceded control over the affairs of state and economy, education, and other institutional areas, but the family, sexuality, and the private sphere generally—the wellspring of moral discipline in society—have remained heavily under their influence.[11]

The rise of the Moral Majority and special interest single-issue politics was the consequence of this reassertion.

Since that time, the traditional evangelical viewpoints on sexuality and marriage have been lost within the broader culture. It should come as no surprise that the 2016 election involved a populist uprising, to "Make America Great Again." It should also be no surprise that evangelicals were strongly supportive of Donald Trump's presidential bid. For Trump reiterated repeatedly the language of the evangelical habitus: American exceptionalism, nativist populism, cultural resentment, and political reassertion. As was pointed out in the "2016 Survey of American Political Culture," "If Trump didn't exist, we would have to invent him."[12] This report also suggests that this election cycle is not an anomaly, and that we are likely to see many more elections like 2016. Nonetheless, it is fair to observe that Trump is "weather" not "climate," and that the long-term culture shift about which this book is focused points in another direction.

This fact may elicit a collective groan. Hunter points out the cultural continuity of this election cycle. And since habitus are historically derived, largely unconscious, and taken for granted, they are not easily changed. These factors do not bode well for American institutional evangelicalism. One must acknowledge that there are troubling features of the evangelical habitus. Doubling down on it, as Trump has done, does not make things any better.

If evangelical behavior in public is reflective of their habitus, and its habitus is a serious source of its public problem, then from a merely sociological perspective, believers like me could become very discouraged.

But who has largely rejected the evangelical habitus without necessarily rejecting an evangelical faith? The answer is believing evangelical millennial New Copernicans!

The rise of evangelical New Copernicans could not be better timed. They are both the future and the potential restorers of the

American evangelical church. Deborah Jian Lee paints the picture of this potential future in her book, *Rescuing Jesus: How People of Color, Women & Queer Christians Are Reclaiming Evangelicalism.*[13] It is clear that the game has changed, that we are living through a significant frame shift. There is a growing literature of young people guiding others on how to navigate this transition. We need to listen to them carefully and not get hung up on minor points of theological disagreement so that we are not able to see the forest for the trees. These are the church's prophetic crap detectors. While many older traditional evangelical leaders may be concerned with aspects of their theological drift or lifestyle choices, they collectively illustrate a changing frame. One thinks of Sarah Bessey's *Out of Sorts: Making Peace with an Evolving Faith,* Rachel Held Evans's *Searching for Sunday: Loving, Leaving, and Finding the Church,* Jen Hatmaker's *Interrupted: When Jesus Wrecks Your Comfortable Christianity,* and Nadia Bolz-Weber's *Accidental Saints: Finding God in All the Wrong People.*[14] It is their shared frame that is the most instructive.

How we decide to respond to the warning discussed here will determine the future direction and viability of the evangelical church. If we continue to play the game according to the old paradigm and habitus, we will be left holding a losing hand and will look the part of the fool. There is still time to acknowledge this frame shift, but the window for making this change is closing fast, as a growing number of young people will no longer have patience with those who continue in the closed transcendent social imaginary.

TAKEAWAYS FROM CHAPTER TWENTY-FIVE

- Habitus are historically derived dispositions of thought and practice, the deep unconscious assumptions about how one successfully navigates social life within a given field.
- Evangelicals act in public not on the basis of their theology, but on the basis of their habitus.
- The American evangelical habitus is shaped by five characteristics, each reflective of a particular period of American history: reign, revival, resentment, retreat, and reassertion.
- There are troubling features of the American evangelical habitus.
- Believing evangelical New Copernicans reject the traditional evangelical habitus and are thus well positioned to provide future leadership in the church.
- If evangelicals continue to engage culture from within their historic habitus, they will be engaging culture with a losing hand.

DISCUSSION QUESTIONS FOR CHAPTER TWENTY-FIVE

- Why is habitus so determinative?
- Why is habitus so difficult to change?
- Which of these habitus, if any, do you find most appealing?
- What are some of the problems with the current evangelical habitus? How would you move away from them?

TWENTY-SIX

PAN-PAN

NEW COPERNICAN FRAME SHIFT AHEAD!

The motivations for our concern will differ. Church leaders recognize that the church as we know it cannot hope to survive without grappling to reach millennials. Parents long to understand and better appreciate their millennial children. And millennials simply want to be taken seriously and finally be respected for who they really are instead of being seen through the lens of pejorative stereotypes.

Things will change. Things are changing. The only question is how we will navigate this change. The pan-pan warning has been given. A new course is being set. Will it be an incremental change in course—to a more southerly route as was the judgment of Captain Smith—or will the response be more comprehensive, seemingly more appropriate to the level of impending peril? As in the case of the *Titanic*, the viability of institutional evangelicalism is in question. As the iceberg of this cultural frame shift isn't going anywhere, the only question is how soon we will have to face it. Short of an immediate emergency "Full stop," all evangelical pastors and para-church leaders need to give careful consideration as to appropriate action. This is what strategic, forward-thinking leadership demands.

There are several obvious steps we will need to take. *First is acknowledging the problem.* The church is potentially losing the next generation of young people. We are struggling to maintain a civil relationship with our millennial children. Parents everywhere are struggling to pass on their love of Jesus and the church to their children. Church youth groups even seem to be aggravating the problem. What we are currently doing is clearly not working on the basis of a host of metrics.

Second, we need to assess our options. One option is that we do nothing and proceed on as if this frame shift is not taking place. We can rationalize this by doubling down on our certainty of ancient truths, long-established traditions, and biblical absolutes. We can harden our stance, and in the face of this "apparent progressive accommodation" to culture, this "drift toward liberalism," resist change with the pride of being a faithful, if diminished, remnant. With a posture of self-confident denial, we can avoid the complex-ities of navigating the institutional stresses of affirming this new frame. We can avoid the pragmatic challenge of potentially losing one's job or congregation. We can question the data or the credibil-ity of the messenger from the safety of our own study. This is the easiest course of action, at least in the short term. But the conse-quences of inaction will soon catch up with us. At that point we will be left with far fewer options. Denial can quickly become tragic.

On the other hand, we can enthusiastically embrace this shift wholeheartedly and naively fail to recognize that such acceptance will require bringing along all of our institutional stakeholders. This error is the tendency of the young. We can be so self-confident in the rightness of the shift that we barrel ahead without sensitivity to the institutional realities and stakeholders (particularly financial) that will need to be convinced to join us. Paradigm shifts are tricky and fraught with institutional challenges. Many have lost their ministry or have been metaphorically burned at the stake for less. Galileo's house arrest is a historically instructive reminder.[1] Wisdom is beneficial. Addressing these challenges will take patience.

Third, we can take cautious, incremental steps in this new direction. This is the approach I recommend. Focus initially on becoming the kind of person that New Copernicans would find an authentic example of faith, someone they would feel comfortable turning to with their most pressing questions. Establish incremental benchmarks. Test the ideas in this book out with millennials in your congregation. Read the book together with them and listen to their responses. Interview nonbelieving millennial New Copernicans. After listening intently to millennial voices, make a commitment to take at least one step in this direction for six months and then assess the results. There is a lot to take in here, and the process for personal and institutional transformation will necessarily be slow and incremental. It's itself an adventure.

This book is nothing more than an invitation to begin a journey of transformation. Paradigm shifts are notoriously difficult, and even more so when the older paradigm is bolstered with a theological rationale. It may feel at first as if you are wandering off the orthodox reservation, even if this is not the case. Attending to the shift and listening with an open mind will go a long way toward avoiding a crisis.

We need the courage to listen and follow the Holy Spirit's guiding prayerful presence. Some additional background reading may be useful, particularly in James K. A. Smith, Iain McGilchrist, and

Lesslie Newbigin's writings. Regularly listening to millennials as a learner—rather than as a pastor or parent—is always advised.

There are opportunity costs to this adventure. You need to consider carefully what will happen if you do nothing. Some cultural conditions will soften the blow. There is a large enough closed transcendent religious audience, particularly in the South, that you can often continue on with little decrease in congregational size. The congregation may age. Sometimes this mutual aging is comfortable, too comfortable, because we agree with each other and so nothing really has to change. The church becomes a self-reinforcing echo chamber. This is the pattern of slow demise and decline. This is the most likely scenario for the evangelical church.

What will change are the legacies you leave behind in your ministry and with your children. You will be moving further and further away from the cultural front lines until you finally are left in a gated community of aging, retired believers who are dwindling in number and relevance. We should do better than this. There is no need to sleepwalk into the future when this pan-pan warning provides the time necessary to respond. We simply need to seize the opportunity and to be grateful for it. A mayday distress call is not inevitable. Take heed—there is a significant cultural frame shift ahead.

And for those who wander and are spiritually frustrated and homeless, you are needed by the church now more than ever. We're listening. Welcome home.

A PRAYER FOR WANDERERS

God of the seekers and the dreamers,
the disaffected and disillusioned,

the worn out and burnt out,
the rejected and leavers . . .

We ask for blessing as we travel, as we doubt, as we
    meander.
We ask for the grace to leave when necessary,
    to come home when we can,
    to create new homes when we need to.

We ask for protection of our souls from those
    who don't understand, who judge, who mock.

We ask for the fortitude to undertake the journey even
    when it's scary
    (or, maybe, especially when it's scary).

We know that as we wander we are not alone
    and as Tolkien says that "Not all who wander are lost."

We know that sometimes we have to leave the confines of
    what we knew
    to see the truth, to hear Your voice, to find out what to
        do next.

We pray You lead us where we need to go, by whatever
    route it takes.
We pray for new ways to see You, to understand new ways
    of being in the world.
We pray for healing and for redemption, and, where
    possible, reconciliation.

We pray for all of this so we can know wholeness, know
our bodies,
know each other, know You.

And be found.[2]

TAKEAWAYS FROM CHAPTER TWENTY-SIX

- The GPS warning has sounded. The only question is how institutional evangelicalism will respond.
- In some sectors of American society, one can do nothing and not experience immediate consequences.
- At issue is not whether there is a frame shift, but how we will respond to it.
- What is being recommended here is to take incremental steps in this new direction. Large, quick changes are not a wise course of action.
- Paradigm shifts are difficult to navigate, especially when the status quo is bolstered with a theological rationale.
- At ultimate issue is the legacy you leave to your millennial children and the legacy of your ministry.
- The New Copernican frame shift is finally a call to a more radical apprenticeship to Jesus and a more accurate assessment of human nature and reality. We do well to celebrate the shift and the millennial carriers of this shift.

DISCUSSION QUESTIONS FOR CHAPTER TWENTY-SIX

- What are three approaches one can take to this frame shift? What approach is being advocated for here?
- Why are paradigm shifts difficult to navigate? Have you navigated them before in your ministry?
- How can you personally change your approach and what steps can you start taking in your church?

ACKNOWLEDGMENTS

It was Isaac Newton who said in a letter to the English polymath Robert Hooke, "If I have seen further it is by standing on the shoulders of giants," or in the Latin: *nanos gigantum humeris insidentes.* Such is the honest case of this book.

The notion that a sixty-year-old, gray-haired traditionalist grandfather would have anything interesting to say about millennials is laughable on the face of it. The combined influences of others simply came together, and out of their unlikely mixture of ideas, temperaments, and experiences emerged this book. I simply gave voice to these disparate muses—the "giants" behind these pages.

Foremost is that of Sir John Templeton—businessman, philanthropist, and Christian mystic. As the former director of cultural engagement at the John Templeton Foundation, I had the weekly task of wrestling with Sir John's enigmatic life and out-of-the-box thinking. He developed a concept of humility-in-theology, which lays the conceptual foundation for these insights about New Copernicans. His belief that there was an inextricable connection between nature and spirituality, between science and religion, had ancient roots in the Celtic spirituality of Saint Patrick of Ireland.

ACKNOWLEDGMENTS

There are two other intellectual giants that I stand on in this book besides Sir John Templeton: neuroscientist Iain McGilchrist and philosopher Charles Taylor. During the course of a single year I was reading the works of all three while focusing my professional attention on the precipitous rise of religious nones, those young people generally characterized as "the spiritually frustrated and homeless." These people are heavily represented in the United States by millennials—the demographic cohort of my three children. This is where my intellectual and spiritual pilgrimage began.

Along the way there have many companions and timely acquaintances who made all the difference. These include Barnaby Marsh, Jim Pitofsky, Charlie Brown, Scott Budnick, Nick Kislinger, Jacob Marshall, Charlie Melcher, Michael Metzger, Dwight Gibson, James Lecesne, Michael Wear, Steven Grabill, James K. A. Smith, James Davison Hunter, and Peter Enns. Each name has its own story. From these early encounters emerged what came to be called the New Copernican thesis. I eventually realized that (1) I was on to something, (2) it needed more research, and (3) I was not automatically a New Copernican.

But intellectual journeys like this also have a spiritual side. There are a number of "soul friends," what the Celtics called an *anamchara*: a friend who serves as mentor, confidant, and confessor, much like an AA sponsor. I owe just as much to these soul friends as I do to the scholars whose work I have relied so heavily upon. My amamchara friends sustained me when insecurity, unemployment, rejection, and disappointment served as life's inevitable speed bumps on the journey. These soul friends include John and Christy Leonard, my colleagues at the Sider Center at Eastern University (Kristyn Komarnicki, Sarah King, Melissa Helmbrecht, Darren Calhoun, Micky Scott Bey Jones, and Ron Sider), and the members of my informal prayer board, a handful of friends who pray for my work with regularity (Art Van Dyck, Pat Van Dyck, and Rochelle Raimao).

There have been others who took the time to read the early manuscript and make perceptive suggestions. These thankfully include Josh Carson, Vanessa Upegui, and MollyGrace Shipman. The master metaphor for the entire book was reworked because of their counsel.

Millennials understand the importance of friends. Academics have gone so far as to say that "dense networks" are the main actors on the stage of cultural change. I am quite certain that this book would not have happened apart from a handful of champions that include John Priddy, Steve Moore, Eric Swanson, Mike McHargue, Andy Hayball, Roxanne Nelson, Tom Scott, Denis Haack, and Chase Daws. One does not make it in this world alone. This book would not have happened without these individuals. It goes without saying that Greg Ligon and LeeEric Fesko from HarperCollins believing in this project turned an idea into a book. Special thanks also to my editor Karin Silver.

Books and academic research always have a thinly veiled biographical backstory. Such is the case here. This book is finally all about my three millennial children—Annie, Dave, and Alex—from whom I have learned so much. They have served on the front line of my crap detectors.

Alex challenged me that if I was going to write in this area that I needed to go to New York to meet with his artistic and social justice–oriented friends. We met in an art gallery in Chelsea where I put forward my thesis. An audience of New York artists and Black Lives Matter activists was not an automatically supportive audience for a grandfather to talk about their age cohort. This thesis has been put through the wringer. I am grateful that we have been getting together regularly since then. I will not be able to leave much to my kids, but I do dedicate my remaining years to empower them and champion their unique perspective. This book is dedicated to them.

And last, but certainly not least, I owe all that I am to the love of my life and best friend, Kathryn. The Philadelphia years have been difficult ones. What is certain is that this book is the fruit of these years and struggles, as it would not have happened without my intense exposure to the thinking of Sir John Templeton. Kathryn, your love and companionship have made this book possible. To Malibu, my English cream golden retriever, I'm grateful for our daily morning walks that have helped clear my head and grounded me in the basic joys of being a dog.

And without trying to be too-pious-by-half, I would be remiss not to mention Jesus, whose reality, love, and providential care is new each day in the details of an enchanted life lived by and for his kingdom. It is for you and your church that this book has been written. Give patience to the skeptical millennial readers and open minds to evangelical pastors. Both will find challenges here.

So this has not been a solitary venture. These are the giants' shoulders on which I now stand. The errors are mine; the insights are ours. The various gifts of your life, love, and prayers have been filtered through my life into this book. Accept my profound gratitude for all you have given me. This book is for you.

David John Seel, Jr.
Erdenheim Farm
Lafayette Hill, Pennsylvania
December 29, 2016

NOTES

FOREWORD

1. Kristina Lizardy-Hajbi, "Engaging Young Adults," Faith Communities Today, accessed April 14, 2017, faithcommunitiestoday.org/sites/default /files/Engaging-Young-Adults-Report.pdf, 2.
2. Michael Lipka, "Why America's 'Nones' Left Religion Behind," Pew Research Center, pewresearch.org/fact-tank/2016/08/24/why -americas-nones-left-religion-behind/.
3. Steve McSwain, "Why Nobody Wants to Go to Church Anymore," *The Huffington Post,* January 23, 2014, huffingtonpost.com/steve -mcswain/why-nobody-wants-to-go-to_b_4086016.html/.
4. John L. Heilbron, *Galileo* (Oxford: Oxford University Press, 2012).
5. "Galileo's Fingers to Be Displayed in Florence Science Museum," *Guardian*, June 8, 2010, theguardian.com/culture/2010/jun/08 /galileo-fingers-museum-florence.
6. "Steve Jobs Narrates 'The Crazy Ones' Think Different Commercial," OSX Daily, October 6, 2011, http://osxdaily.com/2011/10/06/steve-jobs -narrates-the-crazy-ones.

INTRODUCTION

1. As with *mayday, venez m'aidez* ("come to help me"), the emergency call pan-pan derives from French. In French a *panne* ("pan") is a breakdown, such as a mechanical failure. It is the second level of emergency.

2. The real contrasts should not be made with American mainline churches, but with churches in the Global South.

3. 1 Chronicles 12:32.

4. "'Nones' on the Rise," Pew Research Center, October 9, 2012, pewforum.org/2012/10/09/nones-on-the-rise.

5. Drew Dyck, "The Leavers: Young Doubters Exit the Church," *Christianity Today*, November 19, 2010, http://www.christianity today.com/ct/2010/november/27.40.html.

6. Neil Howe and William A. Strauss, *Millennials Rising: The Next Great Generation* (New York: Vintage, 2000).

7. Charles Taylor, *A Secular Age* (Cambridge: Harvard University Press, 2007); James K. A. Smith, *How (Not) to Be Secular: Reading Charles Taylor* (Grand Rapids: Eerdmans, 2014); Iain McGilchrist, *The Master and His Emissary: The Divided Brain and the Making of the Modern World* (New Haven: Yale University Press, 2009); Lesslie Newbigin, *The Gospel in a Pluralistic Society* (Grand Rapids: Eerdmans, 1989); *Proper Confidence: Faith, Doubt & Certainty in Christian Discipleship* (Grand Rapids: Eerdmans, 1995).

PART 1: AN IGNORED WARNING

1. "Mesaba Warned Doomed Titanic of Icebergs," Encyclopedia Titanica, accessed June 12, 2017, encyclopedia-titanica.org/mesaba -warned-doomed-titanic-of-icebergs.html.

CHAPTER 1: SEEING WHILE NOT SEEING

1. C. S. Lewis, "Bluspels and Flalansferes: A Semantic Nightmare," *Selected Literary Essays* (Cambridge: Cambridge University Press, 1969), 265.

2. George Lakoff, *Don't Think of an Elephant!: Know Your Values and Frame the Debate* (White River Junction, VT: Chelsea Green Publishing, 2004), 17.

3. Ibid., 3.

4. Taylor, *A Secular Age*, 171.

5. John Seel, "The World According to Abercrombie & Fitch: What Do Discerning Christians Wear?," *Critique* no. 7, July 7, 2000, http://ransomfellowship.org/wp-content/uploads/2016/10/Critique_2000_07.pdf.

6. Jena McGregor, "Abercrombie & Fitch's Big, Bad Brand Mistake," *Washington Post*, May 22, 2013, https://www.washingtonpost.com/news/on-leadership/wp/2013/05/22/abercrombie-fitchs-big-bad-brand-mistake/.

7. James S. Taylor, *Poetic Knowledge: The Recovery of Education* (Albany: State University of New York, 1998); Karl Stern, *The Flight from Woman* (New York: Farrar, Straus, and Giroux, 1995).

8. Jonathan Haidt, *The Righteous Mind: Why Good People Are Divided by Politics and Religion* (New York: Vintage, 2012); Jonah Lehrer, *Imagine: How Creativity Works* (New York: Houghton Mifflin, 2012).

CHAPTER 2: GETTING THINGS IN FOCUS

1. Thomas Kuhn, *The Structure of Scientific Revolutions* (Chicago: University of Chicago Press, 1970), 113. See also Temple Grandin, *Thinking in Pictures: My Life With Autism* (New York: Vintage, 1995).

2. Walter Isaacson, *Einstein: His Life and Universe* (New York: Simon & Schuster, 2007), 7.

3. Ibid.

4. Owen Gingerich, *The Book Nobody Read: Chasing the Revolutions of Nicolaus Copernicus* (New York: Penguin, 2004).

5. Kuhn, *Structure of Scientific Revolutions*, 85.

6. Ibid., 109.

7. See "The Gaslighting of the Millennial Generation," *Born Again Minimalist* (blog), October 17, 2016, bornagainminimalist.com/2016/10/17/the-gaslighting-of-millennials/.

8. Cole Delbyck, "A CBS Series about Sensitive Millennials Is Already Offending Millennials," *Huffington Post*, August 12, 2016, huffingtonpost.com/entry/a-cbs-series-about-sensitive-millennials-is-already-offending-millennials_us_57ae2ddae4b07184041176ec.

9. Malcolm Venable, "*The Great Indoors* Is More Than Just a

Millennial vs. Gen X Comedy," TVGuide.com, October 25, 2016, tvguide.com/news/the-great-indoors-joel-mchale-cbs-millennials/.

10. Edwin Abbott, *Flatland: A Romance of Many Dimensions* (New York: Dover, 1992).

11. This is why a collaborative ethnography needs to precede survey research. One needs to listen first in order to be able to ask the right questions in the right way.

12. "State Farm® commercial 'Never' (2014)," Vimeo video, 0:31, posted by "marc jacobs," accessed April 15, 2017, vimeo.com/112633967.

13. Lincoln Motor Company Canada, "Matthew McConaughey and the MKC: 'I Just Liked It' Official Commercial," Youtube video, 0:30, posted September 24, 2014, youtube.com/watch?v=VAHiiJ0OPf4.

14. Barbara Herman, "Why Matthew McConaughey's Lincoln Car Ad Is a Big Deal, Signals a Cultural Shift in Ideas about Celebrity, TV's Status, and Commercialism," *International Business Times,* October 17, 2014, ibtimes.com/why-matthew-mcconaugheys -lincoln-car-ad-big-deal-signals-cultural-shift-ideas-about-1707077.

15. Cary Funk and Greg Smith, "'Nones' on the Rise: One-in-Five Adults Have No Religious Affiliation," The Pew Forum on Religion and Public Life, October 9, 2012, 29.

CHAPTER 3: LEFT-BRAIN THINKING

1. Wilhelm Dilthey, *Introduction to the Human Sciences* (Princeton: Princeton University Press, 1991). Quoted in Stern, *Flight from Woman*, 48.

2. McGilchrist, *Master and His Emissary*, 105.

3. Matthew Crawford, *The World Beyond Your Head: On Becoming an Individual in an Age of Distraction* (New York: Farrar, Straus, and Giroux, 2015), 22. "Let us pause for a moment to let the weirdness of all this sink in. Notice that we have moved from an argument about the illegitimacy of particular political authorities in the seventeenth and eighteenth centuries, to the illegitimacy of the authority of other people in general, to the illegitimacy of the authority of our own experience."

4. Ibid., 438.

5. Ibid., 460.

6. Bob Sample, *The Metaphorical Mind: A Celebration of Creative Consciousness* (Reading, MA: Addison-Wesley Publishing Company, 1976), 26.

7. In addition to McGilchrist, see also Robert A. Burton, *On Being Certain: Believing You Are Right Even When You're Not* (New York: St. Martin's Griffin, 2008); Daniel H. Pink, *A Whole New Mind: Why Right-Brainers Will Rule the Future* (New York: Riverhead, 2006); Daniel Kahneman, *Thinking, Fast and Slow* (New York: Farrar, Straus, and Giroux, 2011); William Duggan, *Strategic Intuition: The Creative Spark in Human Achievement* (New York: Columbia Business School Press, 2007); Jamie Holmes, *Nonsense: The Power of Not Knowing* (New York: Crown, 2015).

8. The "medieval synthesis" refers to the idea that under the sovereignty of God, things moderns see as distinct, the medieval perspective saw as unified, such as faith and reason, church and state, belief and the arts, and discipleship and citizenship. This synthesis is primarily attributed to Thomas Aquinas.

9. For a detailed study of these dynamics see Robert Wuthnow's *Communities of Discourse: Ideology and the Social Structures in the Reformation, the Enlightenment, and European Socialism* (Cambridge: Harvard University Press, 1989).

10. Newbigin, *Proper Confidence*, 33.

11. McGilchrist, *Master and His Emissary*, 428.

12. Michael Lewis, *The Big Short: Inside the Doomsday Machine* (New York: Norton, 2011).

13. McGilchrist, *Master and His Emissary*, 429.

14. Ibid., 430.

15. See James K. A. Smith, *Desiring the Kingdom: Worship, Worldview, and Cultural Formation* (Grand Rapids: Baker Academic, 2009) and *Imagining the Kingdom: How Worship Works* (Grand Rapids: Baker Academic, 2013).

CHAPTER 4: FUGITIVES IN THE PEW

1. Christine Barton, Lara Koslow, and Christine Beauchamp, "How Millennials Are Changing the Face of Marketing Forever," *BCG Perspectives*, January 15, 2014, https://www.bcgperspectives.com /content/articles/marketing_center_consumer_customer_insight _how_millennials_changing_marketing_forever/.

2. "So How Many Millennials Are There in the US, Anyway? (Updated)," Marketing Charts, May 3, 2016, marketingcharts.com/traditional/so -how-many-millennials-are-there-in-the-us-anyway-30401/.

3. "Preparing Millennials for a $30 Trillion Wealth Transfer," *Wall Street Journal*, April 27, 2016, http://www.wsj.com/video/preparing -millennials-for-a-30-trillion-wealth-transfer/BD7630BC-2A42 -42ED-B921-51DFFE9F6F48.html.

4. *Making Space for Millennials: A Blueprint for Your Culture, Ministry, Leadership, and Facilities* (Ventura, CA: Barna, 2014).

5. David Kinnaman, *You Lost Me: Why Young Christians Are Leaving the Church . . . and Rethinking Faith* (Grand Rapids: Baker Books, 2011), 59–71.

6. Peter Enns, *The Sin of Certainty: Why God Desires Our Trust More Than Our "Correct" Beliefs* (New York: HarperOne, 2016).

7. Dyck, "The Leavers."

8. James Emery White, *The Rise of the Nones: Understanding and Reaching the Religiously Unaffiliated* (Grand Rapids: Baker Books, 2014).

9. Betsy Cooper et al., "Exodus: Why Americans Are Leaving Religion— and Why They're Unlikely to Come Back," Public Religion Research Institute, September 22, 2016, https://www.prri.org/research/prri-rns -poll-nones-atheist-leaving-religion/. See also Robert Jones, *The End of White Christian America* (New York: Simon & Schuster, 2016).

10. You might consider introducing them to *The Liturgists* podcast and the work of Mike McHargue, aka "Science Mike," theliturgists.com /podcast/, or Krista Tippett's NPR show *On Being*, onbeing.org/.

CHAPTER 5: VOTING WITH ONE'S FEET

1. Peter Berger, *The Sacred Canopy: Elements of a Sociological Theory of Religion* (New York: Anchor, 1969), 138.

2. Cooper et al., "Exodus."

3. Emma Green, "How Will Young People Choose Their Religion?" *Atlantic*, March 20, 2016, https://www.theatlantic.com/politics/archive /2016/03/how-will-young-people-choose-their-religion/474366/.

4. Berger, *Sacred Canopy*, 153. While Berger's point stands, I am not here advocating accommodation for the sake of accommodation or market relevance, but because the New Copernican shift is an improvement, a better understanding of reality, and in this sense a more biblical perspective.

5. Clio Chang, "How the Olympics Lost Millennials," *New Republic*, August 17, 2016, https://newrepublic.com/article/136096/olympics -lost-millennials.

6. If *only* millennials had voted in the 2016 election, it shows the Democratic candidate with a massive advantage over the Republican candidate in the Electoral College: 504 to 23. Samantha McDonald, "Here's What It Would Look Like If Only Millennials Voted," TheZoeReport.com, November 9, 2016, notey.com/@thezoereport _unofficial/external/12663217/this-is-what-would%E2%80%99ve -happened-if-only-millennials-voted.html.

7. Lisa Quast, "Reverse Mentoring: What It Is and Why It Is Beneficial," *Forbes,* January 3, 2011, https://www.forbes.com/sites /work-in-progress/2011/01/03/reverse-mentoring-what-is-it-and -why-is-it-beneficial/#74c1d9d621cc.

PART 2: SIZING UP THE IMPENDING FRAME SHIFT

1. "There are smaller pieces of ice known as 'bergy bits' and 'growlers.' Bergy bits and growlers can originate from glaciers or shelf ice, and may also be the result of a large iceberg that has broken up. A bergy bit is a medium to large fragment of ice. Its height is generally greater than three feet but less than 16 feet above sea level and its area is normally about 1,076–3,229 square feet. Growlers are smaller fragments of ice and are roughly the size of a truck or grand piano. They extend less than three feet above the sea surface and occupy an area of about 215 square feet." "What Is an Iceberg?," National Ocean Service, accessed June 12, 2017, oceanservice.noaa.gov/facts/iceberg.html.

CHAPTER 6: THE VISIBLE SHIFT

1. Crouch, "Stop Engaging 'The Culture.'"
2. The actual quote: "Cultural influence is not measured by the size of one's organizations or by the quantity of one's output, but by the extent to which one's definition of reality is realized—and taken seriously and acted upon by actors in the social world." James Davison Hunter, "Religion, Knowledge, and Power in the Modern Age," unpublished paper, 18.
3. Dallas Willard, *The Renovation of the Heart: Putting on the Character of Christ* (Colorado Springs: NavPress, 2002), 100.
4. Joseph Rentz and Fred Reynolds, "Separating Age, Cohort, and Period Effects in Consumer Behavior," *Advances in Consumer Research 8*: 596–601.
5. Hyperpluralism is the state in which many groups or factions are so strong that one is acutely aware of difference and social cohesion is weakened.
6. Charles Taylor, *The Ethics of Authenticity* (Cambridge: Harvard University Press, 1995), 37.
7. I am not prepared to draw conclusions about the reach of this shift globally. Is it the same in Europe or Asia? I do not know. However, I do think that we will see strong continuities between millennials and Gen Z, the generational cohort after them. Gen Z, with their differences, tend to be millennials on steroids.
8. While these will be obliquely touched on in this book, analyzing these three factors is the subject of another book or books. It would require extensive historical analysis. Causative arguments are much more difficult to make. There also may be additional factors beyond these three, which are merely suggestive.

CHAPTER 7: ALL WHO WANDER ARE NOT LOST

1. Rick Lyman, "Not All Will Follow This Star in the East," *New York Times,* July 4, 2014, nytimes.com/2014/07/05/world/europe/the-rev -tomas-halik-castigates-putin-for-russias-seizure-of-crimea.html.
2. This is a point that is illustrated in Tony Campolo and Bart

Campolo's *Why I Left, Why I Stayed: Conversations on Christianity Between an Evangelical Father and His Humanist Son* (New York: HarperOne, 2017) and is critiqued by theological firebrand Peter Rollins in *The Idolatry of God: Breaking Our Addiction to Certainty and Satisfaction* (New York: Howard Books, 2013).

3. John Templeton, *The Humble Approach: Scientists Discover God* (Philadelphia: Templeton Foundation Press, 1998).

4. "One of the reasons postmodernism has been the bogeyman for the Christian church is that we have become so thoroughly modern. But while postmodernism may be the enemy of our modernity, it can be an ally of our ancient heritage." This is also why the "ancients," such as Celtic Christianity, have such an important contemporary missiological relevance. James K. A. Smith, *Who's Afraid of Postmodernism? Taking Derrida, Lyotard, and Foucault to Church* (Grand Rapids: Baker Academic, 2006), 23.

5. James K. A. Smith, *Who's Afraid of Relativism? Community, Contingency, and Creaturehood* (Grand Rapids: Baker Academic, 2013).

6. Ibid., 35. See also Peter Enns, *The Bible Tells Me So—Why Defending Scripture Has Made Us Unable to Read It* (New York: HarperOne, 2015).

7. Enns, *Sin of Certainty*.

8. Robert Wilken, "Tradition and Trust: The Role of Memory in the Christian Intellectual Life," in *The New Religious Humanists: A Reader*, ed. Gregory Wolfe (New York: Free Press, 1997), 53.

9. Michael McHargue, *Finding God in the Waves: How I Lost My Faith and Found It Again Through Science* (New York: Random House, 2016), 141.

10. Michael Polanyi, *The Tacit Dimension* (Chicago: University of Chicago Press, 2009); *Personal Knowledge: Towards a Post-Critical Philosophy* (Chicago: University of Chicago Press, 1974).

11. McGilchrist, *Master and His Emissary*, 136, 137.

12. John Templeton, *Worldwide Laws of Life: 200 Eternal Spiritual Principles* (Philadelphia: Templeton Foundation Press, 1997), 163.

13. Richard Rohr, *Falling Upward: A Spirituality for the Two Halves of Life* (San Francisco: Jossey-Bass, 2011), 10.

14. Academically speaking, the goal is not to embrace the skepticism of postmodernism or the feigned certainty of foundationalism, but the self-reflective humility of critical realism.

CHAPTER 8: EXPERIENCE BEFORE THINKING

1. Blaise Pascal, *Pensées* (New York: Random House, 1941), 95.
2. Roger Hazelton, *Blaise Pascal: The Genius of His Thought* (Philadelphia: Westminster, 1974), 104.
3. James Houston, ed., *The Mind on Fire: An Anthology of the Writings of Blaise Pascal* (Portland: Multnomah, 1989), 15. See also James R. Peters, *The Logic of the Heart: Augustine, Pascal, and the Rationality of Faith* (Grand Rapids: Baker Academic, 2009).
4. Pascal, *Pensées*, 95.
5. Peter Kreeft, *Christianity for Modern Pagans: Pascal's Pensées* (San Francisco: Ignatius Press, 1993), 231–32.
6. McGilchrist, *Master and His Emissary*, 438.
7. Joseph B. Pine II and James H. Gilmore, *The Experience Economy: Work Is Theater & Every Business a Stage* (Boston: Harvard Business School Press, 1999).
8. Joseph B. Pine II and James H. Gilmore, "Welcome to the Experience Economy," *Harvard Business Review,* July–August, 1998.
9. Ibid.
10. Ibid.
11. Joseph B. Pine II and James H. Gilmore, *Authenticity: What Consumers Really Want* (Boston: Harvard Business School Press, 2007).
12. This is the view developed by Erving Goffmann, *Presentation of Self in Everyday Life* (New York: Anchor, 1959).
13. Jane Callahan, "How Millennials Are Driving the Experience Economy," *Relate by Zendesk*, October 12, 2016.
14. iSpot.tv, "2017 Lincoln MKZ AWD TV Commercial, 'It's Like That' Featuring Matthew McConaughey," video, 0.30, accessed Aptil 17, 2017, ispot.tv/ad/AzVP/2017-lincoln-mkz-awd-its-like-that-feat -matthewmcconaughey.
15. Eventbrite, "Millennials: Fueling the Experience Economy,"

accessed June 12, 2017, eventbrite.com/blog/academy/millennials
-fueling-experience-economy/.

16. Ryan Lamppa, "2014 State of the Sport—Part 1: Non-Traditional
Running Events," *Running USA*, April 27, 2014, http://www.runningusa
.org/index.cfm?fuseaction=runningusawire.details&ArticleId=2941.

17. "A thoughtful engagement with postmodernism will encourage us
to look backward. We will see that much that goes under the banner
of postmodern philosophy has one eye on ancient and medieval
sources and constitutes a significant recovery of premodern ways
of knowing, being, and doing. Ancient and medieval sources
provide a useful countervoice to modernity." Smith, *Who's Afraid of
Postmodernism?*, 25.

18. Matthew Lee Anderson, *Earthen Vessels: Why Our Bodies Matter to
Our Faith* (Minneapolis: Bethany House, 2011); Philip Lee, *Against
the Protestant Gnostics* (Cambridge: Oxford University Press, 1987).

CHAPTER 9: CRACKS IN THE WALL

1. Smith, *How (Not) to Be Secular*, 95.

2. McGilchrist, *Master and His Emissary*, 460.

3. James E. Taylor, "The New Atheists," Internet Encyclopedia of
Philosophy, accessed June 12, 2017, iep.utm.edu/n-atheis/.

4. See Sam Harris, *Waking Up: A Guide to Spirituality Without Religion*
(New York: Simon & Schuster, 2014).

5. Berger, *Sacred Canopy*, 134.

6. Peter Berger, *A Rumor of Angels: Modern Society and the Rediscovery
of the Supernatural* (New York: Anchor, 1970).

7. Smith, *How (Not) to Be Secular*, 73.

8. Julian Barnes, *Nothing to Be Frightened Of* (New York: Vintage, 2008), 3.

9. Frank Schaeffer is an artist and writer who is the son of the late
evangelical apologist and missionary Francis A. Schaeffer.

10. Elizabeth Gilbert, *Big Magic: Creative Living Beyond Fear* (New
York: Riverhead, 2015), 34.

11. The theme of Burning Man 2017 is "Radical Ritual."

12. From the cover of Rachelle Mee-Chapman's book, *Relig-ish*: "When

it comes to religion, 'choose one' is no longer your only option. You can be spiritual-but-not-religious or not particularly religious at all yet still have a robust system of beliefs and values that guides you. Creating your own set of eclectic spiritual practices is not a sign that you are a faith-less person but rather a faithful person responding with honesty to an increasingly expanding world. If faithfully attending church isn't helping you live out your values in everyday ways, becoming relig-ish may be the answer!" Rachelle Mee-Chapman, *Relig-ish: Soulful Living in a Spiritual-But-Not-Religious World* (Atlanta: Chalice Press, 2016).

13. See Devin Brown, *A Life Observed: A Spiritual Biography of C. S. Lewis* (Grand Rapids: Brazos, 2013), and Gregory S. Cootsona, *C. S. Lewis and the Crisis of a Christian* (Louisville: Westminster John Knox Press, 2014).

14. McHargue, *Finding God in the Waves*. See also "New Copernicans Episode 11: Mystical Experience," Windrider Institute, July 19, 2015, windriderforum.info/portfolio_page/episode-11-mystical-experience/.

15. Nicholas Kristof, "Am I a Christian, Pastor Timothy Keller?" *New York Times*, December 23, 2016, https://www.nytimes.com/2016/12/23/opinion/sunday/pastor-am-i-a-christian.html.

16. Rachel Held Evans, *Searching for Sunday: Loving, Leaving, and Finding the Church* (Nashville: Nelson, 2015); Enns, *Sin of Certainty*; and Frank Schaeffer, *Why I Am an Atheist Who Believes in God: How to Give Love, Create Beauty, and Find Peace* (Salisbury, MA: Regina Orthodox, 2014).

17. Such as the listeners of *The Liturgists* podcast (theliturgists.com/podcast) and *Ask Science Mike* (mikemchargue.com/ask-science-mike/).

18. Funk and Smith, "'Nones' on the Rise," 16.

CHAPTER 10: SELF-RIGHTEOUS BLINDNESS

1. Smith, *Who's Afraid of Postmodernism?*

2. Ibid., 25.

3. Ibid., 117. By "Cartesian anxiety," Smith means the assumptions of certainty bequeathed us by the Enlightenment project and

left-brained thinking: "A properly postmodern theology will refuse the terms of the debate set by Descartes at the origins of modernity."

4. Ibid., 119. I personally follow the theological orientation of James K. A. Smith as outlined in his book *Introducing Radical Orthodoxy: Mapping a Post-Secular Theology* (Grand Rapids: Baker Academic, 2004). There is a growing literature by those who have experienced forms of spiritual abuse. See Stephen Arterburn and Jack Felton, *Toxic Faith: Experiencing Healing from Painful Spiritual Abuse* (Colorado Springs: Shaw, 2001).

5. "From Augustine through Aquinas, medieval theologians were very attentive to the difference between 'comprehending' God (which was impossible) and 'knowing' God (which was possible, because God had given himself to us in terms that could be received). Why should we think that the criterion for knowledge is godlike certainty or omniscience?" Smith, *Who's Afraid of Postmodernism?*, 120.

6. Tracy Balzer, *Thin Places: An Evangelical Journey into Celtic Christianity* (Abilene, TX: Leafwood Publishers, 2007), and Esther de Waal, *Celtic Light: A Tradition Rediscovered* (London: Fount, 1997).

7. Paul Valley, "Pope Francis: Not So Much a Reformer as a Revolutionary," *Independent,* September 27, 2013.

8. Pope Francis, *The Joy of Love* (*Amoris Laetitia*): *On Love in the Family* (New York: Paulist Press, 2016).

9. Samuel G. Freedman, "Focus on the Family Works to Change Its Message," *New York Times,* March 9, 2013, http://www.nytimes.com /2013/03/09/us/focus-on-the-family-transforms-its-message.html.

10. Christopher West, *Heaven's Song: Sexual Love as It Was Meant to Be* (West Chester, PA: Ascension Press, 2008), 25.

11. This story focuses on a lavish dinner that a French servant woman named Babette prepares for a group of pious ascetics in an isolated Norwegian village on Sunday, December 15, 1883. If you haven't seen this film, I highly recommend it. It does the film a disservice to discuss its plot in too much detail. It needs to be experienced, not talked about.

12. Megan DeFranza, "Disappearing Our Pastors," The BTS Center, June 3, 2016, thebtscenter.org/disappearing-our-pastors/.

CHAPTER 11: RELIGIOUSLY TONE-DEAF

1. Richard Dawkins, *The God Delusion* (Boston: Mariner, 2008); Christopher Hitchens, *God Is Not Great: How Religion Poisons Everything* (New York: Twelve, 2009); Sam Harris, *The End of Faith: Religion, Terror, and the Future of Reason* (New York: Norton, 2005); and Daniel Dennett, *Breaking the Spell: Religion as a Natural Phenomenon* (New York: Penguin, 2007).

2. Dawkins, *God Delusion*, 150.

3. Mark Noll, *The Scandal of the Evangelical Mind* (Grand Rapids: Eerdmans, 1995), 3.

4. Reza Aslan, "Harris, Hitchens, Dawkins, Dennett: Evangelical Atheists?" *On Faith* (blog), July 16, 2010, onfaith.co/onfaith/2010 /07/16/harris-hitchens-dawkins-dennett-evangelical-atheists/929. This contrast is also seen in Tony and Bart Campolo's *Why I Left, Why I Stayed*.

5. Glenn Olsen, *The Turn to Transcendence: The Role of Religion in the Twenty-First Century* (Washington, DC: Catholic University of America Press, 2010).

6. McGilchrist notes the contrast between the academic disciplines of physics and biology. "There is a tendency for the life sciences to consider a mechanistic universe more 'real,' even though physics long ago moved away from this legacy of nineteen-century materialism, with the rather odd result that the inanimate universe has come to appear animate, to take part in mind, while the animate universe appears inanimate, mindless." McGilchrist, *Master and His Emissary*, 177. See also Adam Frank, "Minding Matter," *Aeon*, March 13, 2017, aeon.co/essays/materialism-alone-cannot-explain-the-riddle-of-consciousness/: "We know that matter remains mysterious just as mind remains mysterious, and we don't know what the connections between those mysteries should be. Classifying consciousness as a material problem is tantamount to saying that consciousness, too, remains fundamentally unexplained."

7. For more on this subject, see Marcelo Gleiser, *The Island of Knowledge: The Limits of Science and the Search for Meaning* (New

York: Basic, 2014); Robert Crease and Alfred Goldhaber, *The Quantum Moment: How Planck, Bohr, Einstein, and Heisenberg Taught Us to Love Uncertainty* (New York: Norton, 2014); and David Skeel, *True Paradox: How Christianity Makes Sense of Our Complex World* (Downers Grove, IL: InterVarsity Press, 2014).

8. Burton, *On Being Certain*, xiv. And from p. xiii: "Despite how certainty feels, it is neither a conscious choice nor even a thought process. Certainty and similar states of 'knowing what we know' arise out of involuntary brain mechanisms that like love or anger, function independently of reason." See also Kahneman, *Thinking Fast and Slow*.

9. McHargue, *Finding God in the Waves*.

10. Chris Stedman, *Faitheist: How an Atheist Found Common Ground with the Religious* (Boston: Beacon, 2012), 146.

11. Thomas Nagel, *Mind & Cosmos: Why the Materialist Neo-Darwinian Conception of Nature Is Almost Certainly False* (Cambridge: Oxford University Press, 2012).

12. Ibid., 7.

13. Max Jammer, *Einstein and Religion* (Princeton: Princeton University Press, 1999), 7. See also Virginia Stem Owen, *And the Trees Clap Their Hands: Faith, Perception, and the New Physics* (Eugene, OR: Wipf & Stock, 2005); and Krista Tippett, *Einstein's God: Conversations About Science and the Human Spirit* (New York: Penguin, 2010).

CHAPTER 12: HAUNTED DOUBTERS

1. George Ritzer, *Sociological Theory* (New York: Alfred A. Knopf, 1983), 129.

2. Nick Bilton, "A Line Is Drawn in the Desert," *New York Times*, August 20, 2014, https://www.nytimes.com/2014/08/21/fashion/at-burning-man-the-tech-elite-one-up-one-another.html.

3. Burning Man (website), accessed June 12, 2017, burningman.org/.

4. Rachel Bowditch, *On the Edge of Utopia: Performance and Ritual at Burning Man* (Chicago: University of Chicago Press, 2010); Wendy Clupper, "The Performance Culture of Burning Man" (PhD diss.,

University of Maryland, 2007); Lee Gilmore, *Theatre in a Crowded Fire: Ritual and Spirituality at Burning Man* (Berkeley: University of California Press, 2010).

5. "The 10 Principles of Burning Man," accessed April 18, 2017, burningman.org/culture/philosophical-center/10-principles/.

6. See *Spark: A Burning Man Story*, documentary film, 2013, website accessed April 18, 2017, sparkpictures.com/.

7. Larry Harvey, "Radical Ritual: Spirit and Soul," *The Burning Man Journal*, January 30, 2017, journal.burningman.org/2017/01 /philosophical-center/spirituality/radical-ritual-spirit-and-soul/.

8. Smith, *How (Not) to Be Secular*, 141.

9. Taylor, *A Secular Age*, 423–535.

10. Smith, *How (Not) to Be Secular*, 142.

11. Ibid., 143.

12. Seth Godin, "None of the Above," *Seth's Blog*, April 8, 2016, sethgodin.typepad.com/seths_blog/2016/04/none-of-the-above.html.

13. Taylor, *A Secular Age*, 73.

14. David Dark, *Life's Too Short to Pretend You're Not Religious* (Downers Grove, IL: InterVarsity, 2016).

15. Nancy Ammerman, "Spiritual But Not Religious? Beyond Binary Choices in the Study of Religion," *Journal for the Scientific Study of Religion* 52, no. 2 (2013): 258–78.

16. Linda Mercadante, *Belief Without Borders: Inside the Minds of the Spiritual But Not Religious* (Cambridge: Oxford University Press, 2014), 53–66.

17. Ibid., 75.

18. Ibid., 251.

19. Cooper et al., "Exodus."

20. Funk and Smith, "'Nones' on the Rise," 16.

21. Smith, *How (Not) to Be Secular*, 9.

22. Eventbrite, "Millennials," 2.

23. "Untitled Post," *Love, Life, and Video Games* (blog), accessed April 18, 2017, category5kawaiiju.tumblr.com/post/156402871570/tlatotem -animar-smol-of-elephants/.

CHAPTER 13: HUMILITY IN THEOLOGY

1. Stephen G. Post, *Is Ultimate Reality Unlimited Love?* (Philadephia: Templeton Foundation Press, 2014).
2. Rohr, *Falling Upward*, 10.
3. C. S. Lewis, *The Pilgrim's Regress* (Grand Rapids: Eerdmans, 1992), 204.
4. McHargue, *Finding God in the Waves*, 226.
5. Lewis, *Pilgrim's Regress*, 149. The gorge is the gulf between nonfaith and faith. Lewis argues here that the road back to faith is through the church, "Mother Kirk." He outlines the pagan conversion process: "What is universal is not the particular picture, but the arrival of some message, not perfectly intelligible, which wakes this desire and sets men to longing for something East or West of the world; something possessed, if at all, only in the act of desiring it, and lost so quickly that the craving itself becomes craved; something that tends inevitably to be confused with common or even with vile satisfactions lying close to hand, yet which is able, if any man faithfully live through the dialectic of its successive births and deaths, to lead him at last where true joys are to be found." Ibid., 151.
6. Anne Lamott, *Traveling Mercies: Some Thoughts on Faith* (New York: Anchor, 1999), 3. "My coming to faith did not start with a leap but rather a series of staggers from what seemed like one safe place to another."
7. Templeton, *The Humble Approach*; and John Marks Templeton and Robert L. Hermann, *Is God the Only Reality?: Science Points to a Deeper Meaning of the Universe* (Philadelphia: Templeton Foundation Press, 2012).
8. A quick summary of his conversion story can be found at: "New Copernicans Episode 11: Mystical Experience," Windrider Institute, July 19, 2015, windriderforum.info/portfolio_page/episode-11-mystical -experience/.
9. Bart Campolo, who is older than a millennial, is clearly an exception.
10. Wild Goose Festival (website), accessed June 12, 2017, http:// wildgoosefestival.org/.
11. Tippett, *Einstein's God*.

12. Geron Porphyrios, *Wounded by Love* (Limni: Denise Harvey, 2005), 107. McGilchrist adds, "Most forms of imagination or of innovation, intuitive problem solving, spiritual thinking, or artistic creativity require us to transcend language, at least language in the accepted sense of a referential code." He also argues in this same vein that, historically and developmentally, music preceded language. McGilchrist, *Master and His Emissary*, 107.

13. Rohr, *Falling Upward*.

14. Dalai Lama, *Beyond Religion: Ethics for the Whole World* (Boston: Mariner, 2012). This book is a manifesto for New Copernican spirituality.

CHAPTER 14: SECULAR

1. Brian Baker, "Return from Burning Man 2," September 11, 2016, sermon at Trinity Cathedral, Vimeo video, 23:00, vimeo.com/182429332.

2. Smith, *How (Not) to Be Secular*, 142.

3. Ibid., 140.

4. Smith, *Desiring the Kingdom*, and *You Are What You Love: The Spiritual Power of Habit* (Grand Rapids: Brazos, 2016).

5. For more on the apologetics of the imagination, see Brian Godawa, *Word Pictures: Knowing God through Story & Imagination* (Downers Grove, IL: InterVarsity Press, 2009); John Montgomery ed., *Myth, Allegory and Gospel: An Interpretation of J. R. R. Tolkien, C. S. Lewis, G. K. Chesterton, and Charles Williams* (Minneapolis: Bethany, 1974); James W. Sire, *Apologetics Beyond Reason: Why Seeing Really Is Believing* (Downers Grove, IL: InterVarsity Press, 2014); and Smith, *Imagining the Kingdom*.

6. Joseph Campbell, *The Hero with a Thousand Faces* (Novato, CA: New World, 2008). Joseph Campbell was an American mythologist best known for this book, in which he discusses his theory of the journey of the archetypal hero found in world mythologies.

7. Joseph Campbell, *The Power of Myth* (New York: Anchor, 1991); *The Masks of God* (New York: Penguin, 1976); Edith Hamilton, *Mythology: Timeless Tales of Gods and Heroes* (New York: Mentor, 1969).

8. Mark Rodgers, "Comic-Con and the Modern Myth," *Wedgewood Circle*, August 5, 2016, claphamgroup.com/featured/comic-con-part-2/; Neil Gaiman, *American Gods* (New York: William Morrow, 2016).

9. James W. Sire, *Echoes of a Voice: We Are Not Alone* (Grand Rapids: InterVarsity Press, 2014); *Apologetics: Beyond Reason*.

10. David Abram, *The Spell of the Sensuous* (New York: Random House, 1996), 22. "The simple premise of this book is that we are human only in contact, and conviviality, with what is not human."

11. Carl E. Braaten and Robert W. Jenson, *Either/Or: The Gospel or Neopaganism* (Grand Rapids: Eerdmans, 1995), 7. Neo-paganism is a form of pantheism. Pantheism is the broader category.

12. Clotilde Morhan, "Paganism and the Conversion of C. S. Lewis," *Catholic Dossier*, March/April 2005.

13. Having been converted from pantheism, Lewis was well aware of its problems. In "Rejoinder to Dr. Pittenger," *God in the Dock* (Grand Rapids: Eerdmans, 1970), 181, he writes, "I freely admit, that believing in both [transcendence and immanence], I have stressed the transcendence of God more than His immanence. I thought, and think, that the present situation demands this. I see around me no danger of Deism but much of an immoral, naïve, and sentimental pantheism. I have often found that it was in fact the chief obstacle to conversion."

14. Lewis H. Lapham, "She Wants Her TV! He Wants His Book," *Harper's*, March 1993, 44–55. See also John Seel, "Spirituality and Pop Music: From Tori Amos to Lauryn Hill," *Critique* no. 3, 1999.

15. C. S. Lewis, "*De Descriptione Temporum*," in *Selected Literary Essays* (Cambridge: Cambridge University Press, 1969), 4–5.

16. "In one of his *Latin Letters* Lewis speculated that some modern people may need to be brought to pre-Christian pagan insights in preparation for more adequately receiving the Christian gospel." Colin Duriez, "The Romantic Writer: Lewis's Theology of Fantasy," in *The Pilgrim's Guide: C. S. Lewis and the Art of Witness*, ed. David Mills (Grand Rapids: Eerdmans, 1998), 108. See also John Seel, "Meet Your Neighborhood Neopagan," *Re:Generation Quarterly*, Fall 1997.

17. Dallas Willard, *The Divine Conspiracy: Rediscovering our Hidden Life in God* (San Francisco: HarperSanFrancisco, 1998), 82.

18. This is attributed to Pierre Teilhard de Chardin in *The Joy of Kindness*, by Robert J. Furey (New York: Crossroad, 1993), 138; but it is attributed to G. I. Gurdjieff in *Beyond Prophecies and Predictions: Everyone's Guide to the Coming Changes*, by Moira Timms (New York: Ballantine Books, 1993), 62; neither cites a source. It was widely popularized by Wayne Dyer, who often quotes it in his presentations, crediting it to Chardin, as does Stephen Covey in *Living the 7 Habits: Stories of Courage and Inspiration* (New York: Simon & Schuster, 2000), 47.

19. Thomas Molnar, *The Pagan Temptation* (Grand Rapids: Eerdmans, 1987), 164.

20. The corrective to this is a four-chapter gospel: creation, fall, redemption, and restoration.

21. Sarah Withrow King, *Vegangelial: How Caring for Animals Can Shape Your Faith* (Grand Rapids: Zondervan, 2016); and Matthew Scully, *Dominion: The Power of Man, the Suffering of Animals, and the Call to Mercy* (New York: St. Martin's Griffin, 2003).

22. See Leanne Payne, *Real Presence: The Glory of Christ with Us and Within Us* (Grand Rapids: Baker Books, 1995).

23. Edith Schaeffer, *L'Abri* (Wheaton, IL: Crossway, 1992).

CHAPTER 15: EXPLORERS

1. *Wikipedia*, s.v. "Pilgrimage," accessed June 12, 2017, en.wikipedia.org/wiki/Pilgrimage.

2. I am indebted to Chase Daws for this comment and insight.

3. Lucinda Vardey, ed., *Mother Teresa: A Simple Path* (New York: Ballantine, 1995), 90.

4. Gregory Wolfe, *Beauty Will Save the World: Recovering the Human in an Ideological Age* (Wilmington, DE: Intercollegiate Studies Institute, 2011), 240; Malcolm Muggeridge, *Confessions of a Twentieth Century Pilgrim* (New York: Harper Collins, 1988).

5. P. G. Jestice, *Encyclopedia of Irish Spirituality* (Santa Barbara, CA: Clio, 2000), 277.

6. Esther de Waal, *The Celtic Way of Prayer: The Recovery of the Religious Imagination* (New York: Image, 1997), 3.

CHAPTER 16: CROSS-PRESSURED BELIEFS

1. Smith, *How (Not) to Be Secular*, 23. See also John Seel, "Pilgrim Stories: Evangelism Is a Dirty Word to Millennials," *Critique* no. 3, June 27, 2016, http://ransomfellowship.org/wp-content/uploads/2016/10/critique2016-3.pdf.

2. A. J. Swoboda, *The Dusty Ones: Why Wandering Deepens Your Faith* (Grand Rapids: Baker Books, 2016), 4, 5.

3. DeFranza, "Disappearing Our Pastors."

4. Ibid.

5. David Runcorn, *A Center of Quiet: Hearing God When Life Is Noisy* (Downers Grove, IL: InterVarsity Press, 1990), 85.

6. St. John of the Cross, *Dark Night of the Soul* (New York: Dover, 2003); Teresa of Ávila, *Interior Castle* (New York: Image, 2004).

7. Brian Kolodiejchuk, ed., *Mother Teresa: Come Be My Light* (New York: Image, 2009).

CHAPTER 17: EXPERIENTIAL

1. Molly Shea, "Millennials Are Killing Gyms, Too," *New York Post,* October 17, 2016, nypost.com/2016/10/17/millennials-are-killing-gyms-too/.

2. Charley Locke, "Uber, but for Millennials Who Want Orchestras in Their Living Room," *Wired,* October 14, 2016, https://www.wired.com/2016/10/groupmuse-classical-music-concerts/.

3. Ray Oldenburg, *The Great Good Place: Cafes, Coffee Shops, Bookstores, Bars, Hair Salons, and Other Hangouts at the Heart of a Community* (New York: Marlowe & Company, 1999). In community building, the third place is the social surroundings separate from the two usual social environments of home and the office.

4. Emma Green, "The Secret Christians of Brooklyn," *Atlantic,* September 8, 2015, https://www.theatlantic.com/politics/archive /2015/09/st-lydias-microchurch-brooklyn-secret-christians/404119/.

5. Jeremiah Sierra, "Sanctuary in the City: A Dinner Church in Brooklyn," *On Faith,* July 14, 2015, faithstreet.com/onfaith/2014/07/14 /a-dinner-church-finds-a-home-in-brooklyn/33042.

6. C.S. Lewis, *The Four Loves* (New York: Harcourt Brace Jovanovich Publishers, 1988), 66. "We picture lovers face to face but friends side by side; their eyes look ahead."

7. "Denis and Margie Haack," Ransom Fellowship, accessed June 13, 2017, ransomfellowship.org/about/people/dennis-and-margie-haack/.

CHAPTER 18: RELATIONSHIPS

1. "One-third of married couples meet online: study," *NYDailyNews,* June 4, 2013, http://www.nydailynews.com/life-style/one-third -u-s-marriages-start-online-dating-study-article-1.1362743.

2. Deepak Chopra, "LIVE from The Nantucket Project," AOL Build video, 56:29, September 23, 2016, build.aol.com/video/57e55a845095 495a4c5950d0/. Transcribed by author. In one sense, God is the only noun "I am," but he is best understood as a verb, as an ongoing conversation of love. In this vein see Richard Rohr's "law of three" in *Divine Dance: The Trinity and Your Transformation* (New Kensington, PA: Whitaker, 2016); Richard Rohr, "Divine Dance: The Trinity and Your Transformation," Talks at Google, YouTube video, 48:36, posted on November 7, 2016, youtube.com/watch?v=U1rA_gOgcjs.

3. *Coyotaje* is a colloquial Mexican-Spanish term referring to the practice of people smuggling across the US–Mexico border.

4. "AJAM Presents: 'Borderland,'" Aljazeera America, accessed June 13, 2017, america.aljazeera.com/watch/shows/al-jazeera-america -presents-borderland.html/.

5. Oldenburg, *The Great Good Place.*

6. "An Introduction to Q Place," Q Place, video, accessed April 19, 2017, qplace.com.

7. "Tattoos: A Defining Mark for Millennials," Millennial Marketing,

March 2101, millennialmarketing.com/2010/03/tatoos-a-defining-mark-for-millennials/. Close to 40 percent of millennials have a tattoo.

8. Heather Wood Rudúlph, "Why Tattoos Have Become Millennials' Favorite Psychosomatic Healing Modality," *MindBodyGreen*, October 19, 2016, mindbodygreen.com/0-27033/why-tattoos-have -become-millennials-favorite-psychosomatic-healing-modality. html/. See also "Lars Krutak—Tattoo Anthropologist," LarsKrutak .com, accessed April 19, 2017, larskrutak.com/.

9. There are still some culturally accepted practices that Christian missionaries should and do stand against, such as female genital mutilation.

CHAPTER 19: AUTHENTICITY

1. Paul Oestrieicher, *Camelot, Inc.: Leadership and Management Insights from King Arthur and the Round Table* (Santa Barbara, CA: Praeger, 2011) and T. H. White, *The Once and Future King* (New York: Penguin, 2016). This is an insight largely developed by Mike Metzger of The Clapham Institute (claphaminstitute.org).

2. Steven Sample, *The Contrarian's Guide to Leadership* (San Francisco: Jossey-Bass, 2003).

3. James Gilmore and Joseph Pine, *Authenticity: What Consumers Really Want* (Cambridge: Harvard University Press, 2007), 96.

4. Jean Baudrillard, *Simulacra and Simulation* (Ann Arbor: University of Michigan Press, 1994, 1.

5. Mark Sayers, *The Trouble with Paris: Following Jesus in a World of Plastic Promises* (Nashville: Thomas Nelson, 2008).

6. Scott Huddleston, "Alamo Village Closes Indefinitely," *MySA*, August 31, 2010, mysanantonio.com/news/local_news/article/Alamo -Village-closes-indefinitely-638402.php.

7. Ada Louise Huxtable, *The Unreal America: Architecture and Illusion* (New York: The New Press, 1997).

8. Baudrillard, *Simulacra and Simulation*, 19.

9. Gilmore and Pine, *Authenticity*, 97.

10. Charles Drew, *Body Broken: Can Republicans and Democrats Sit in the Same Pew* (Greensboro, NC: New Growth Press, 2012).

11. Yasmine Hafiz, "Boy in Yellow Steals Pope Francis' Heart," *Huffington Post*, October 29, 2013, huffingtonpost.com/2013/10/29/pope-francis-boy-stage-yellow-_n_4175486.html/.

CHAPTER 20: HAUNTED

1. Bruce Marshall, *The World, the Flesh, and Father Smith* (New York: Houghton Mifflin, 1945), 108.

2. Christopher West, *Fill These Hearts: God, Sex, and the Universal Longing* (New York: Image, 2012), 16.

3. C. S. Lewis, *The Weight of Glory* (New York: HarperCollins, 2001), 26.

4. Smith, *Desiring the Kingdom*, 46. See also Smith, *You Are What You Love*.

5. Smith, *Desiring the Kingdom*, 52–53.

6. Ron Martin-Dent, "Letter to the Editor," *The Seattle Times*, September 10, 2016, seattletimes.com/opinion/letters-to-the-editor/millennials-making-the-world-a-better-place/.

7. Balzer, *Thin Places*, 26.

8. N. T. Wright, *Simply Christian: Why Christianity Makes Sense* (San Francisco: HarperSanFrancisco, 2006), x. Because this book updates C. S. Lewis's *Mere Christianity* according to these four portals, it is a valuable tool in reaching New Copernicans.

9. C. S. Lewis, *Mere Christianity* (New York: Macmillan, 1952), 119.

10. Scott Burson and Jerry Walls, *C. S. Lewis and Francis Schaeffer: Lessons for a New Century from the Most Influential Apologists of Our Time* (Downers Grove, IL: InterVarsity Press, 1998), 150.

11. Ibid., 263.

CHAPTER 21: JUSTICE

1. Emily Marks, "The One Question that Can Motivate Millennials," *University Herald*, October 22, 2016, http://www.universityherald.com/articles/45567/20161022/one-question-motivate-millennials.htm.

2. This insight is indebted to Michael Metzger, president of The Clapham Institute, claphaminstitute.org/. These four notes parallel

that of the four-chapter gospel: creation, fall, redemption, and restoration. The tendency to reduce the gospel to two chapters—fall and redemption—is a weakness of the evangelical church. Dallas Willard describes this as the "gospel of sin management" (*The Divine Conspiracy*, 35–59).

3. Russell Berman, "Hillary Clinton's Blunt View of Social Progress," *Atlantic,* August 22, 2015, https://www.theatlantic.com/politics /archive/2015/08/hillary-clintons-blunt-view-of-social-progress /402020/.

4. Eugene Cho, "Ted Williams: The Story Behind His Golden Voice," *Huffington Post,* May 25, 2011, huffingtonpost.com/eugene-cho/ted -williams-the-story-be_b_805090.html.

CHAPTER 22: BEAUTY

1. Thomas Dubay, *The Evidential Power of Beauty: Science and Theology Meet* (San Francisco: Ignatius Press, 1999), 20.

2. Julian Johnson, *Who Needs Classical Music?: Cultural Choice and Musical Value* (Cambridge: Oxford University Press, 2011), 12.

3. Wright, *Simply Christian,* 44.

4. Wolfe, *Beauty Will Save the World,* xiv.

5. Leo Spitzer, *Classical and Christian Ideas of World Harmony* (Baltimore: Johns Hopkins Press, 1963). See also Jeremy Begbie, *Resounding Truth: Christian Wisdom in the World of Music* (Grand Rapids: Baker Academic, 2007); and *Theology, Music and Time* (Cambridge: Cambridge University Press, 2008).

6. Eric Nisenson, *Ascension: John Coltrane and His Quest* (New York: Da Capo Press, 1995), 121.

7. Sørina Higgins, "The Church's Role in Art," *Comment,* May 27, 2011, https://www.cardus.ca/comment/article/2792/the-churchs -role-in-art/. There is much that one can learn from organizations working in this space: The International Arts Movement, Christians in the Visual Arts, The Church and Arts Network, The Christian Artist Network, The Society for the Arts, Religion and Contemporary Culture, The Opiate Mass, and *Image* magazine.

8. Myra Reynolds, *Selections from the Poems and Plays of Robert Browning* (Chicago: Scott, Foresman & Company, 1909), 251.

CHAPTER 23: LOVE

1. Smith, *Desiring the Kingdom*, 50.
2. Vardey, *Mother Teresa*, 79.
3. John Cacioppo and William Patrick, *Loneliness: Human Nature and the Need for Social Connection* (New York: Norton, 2008).
4. West, *Fill These Hearts*, 90.
5. Ibid., 92.
6. "Oriented to Love," Evangelicals for Social Action, accessed April 19, 2017, evangelicalsforsocialaction.org/oriented-to-love/.
7. John Seel, "Sex Points the Way: 'Friends with Benefits' and the Nature of Reality," *Critique* no. 5, October 25, 2011, http://ransomfellowship.org/wp-content/uploads/2016/10/Critique52011.pdf.
8. "This is not an abstraction, for each of these persons is created in the image of God, and thus is in tension because, within himself, there are things which speak of the real world." See Francis Schaeffer, *The God Who Is There* (London: Hodder and Stoughton, 1968), 124.

CHAPTER 24: SPIRIT

1. Dalai Lama, *Beyond Religion*.
2. Laura DaSilva, "Millennials Restoring Their Faith at Toronto's C3 Church," *CBC News,* October 23, 2016, http://www.cbc.ca/news/canada/toronto/millennials-pentecostal-church-movement-toronto-1.3818237.
3. Rachel Held Evans, "Want Millennials Back in the Pews? Stop Trying to Make Church 'Cool,'" *Washington Post,* April 30, 2015, https://www.washingtonpost.com/opinions/jesus-doesnt-tweet/2015/04/30/fb07ef1a-ed01-11e4-8666-a1d756d0218e_story.html?utm_term=.2128b59c05dd.
4. Ibid.
5. John Seel, "Pilgrim Stories: Evangelism Is a Dirty Word to Millennials," *Critique* no. 3, June 27, 2016, http://ransomfellowship.org/wp-content/uploads/2016/10/critique2016-3.pdf.

6. Abraham Joshua Heschel, *Man Is Not Alone: A Philosophy of Religion* (New York: Farrar, Straus, and Giroux, 1976), 174.

7. Craig Bartholomew and Michael Goheen, *The Drama of Scripture: Finding Our Place in the Biblical Story* (Grand Rapids: Baker Academic, 2014), 19.

8. David Williams, "'As You Wish': What *The Princess Bride* Can Tell Us about Reading the Bible Story Well," The Aetherlight, July 2015, unpublished manuscript by Scarlett City Studio, www.theaether light.com.

9. Kate Pickert, "The Mindful Revolution," *Time*, February 3, 2014, http://time.com/1556/the-mindful-revolution/.

10. It should be noted that a Wi-Fi connection is a bidirectional connection in real time with data going in both directions. One can think of it as a "relational" connection.

11. Madeleine L'Engle, *Walking on Water: Reflections on Faith and Art* (New York: Convergent Books, 2016), 140–41.

CHAPTER 25: CHANGING TRUMP CARDS

1. Pierre Bourdieu, *The Logic of Practice* (Stanford: Stanford University Press, 1990), 9.

2. Karl Marx, "The Eighteenth Brumaire of Louis Bonaparte," in *Karl Marx: Selected Writings*, ed. David McLellen (Cambridge: Oxford University Press, 1977), 300.

3. Pierre Bourdieu, *Outline of a Theory of Practice* (Cambridge: Cambridge University Press, 1977), 79.

4. John Seel, *The Evangelical Forfeit: Can We Recover?* (Grand Rapids: Baker Books, 1993); particularly see chapter 2, "Yesterday's Man."

5. Sidney Ahlstrom, *A Religious History of the American People* (New York: Image, 1975), 169.

6. Alexis de Tocqueville, *Democracy in America Volume 1* (New York: Vintage, 1945), 6.

7. Populism, in contrast to elitism, is a belief in the power of regular people, and in their right to have control over their government. Within the church it is associated with the presidency of Andrew

Jackson and the Second Great Awakening (1800–1850). Trump's presidency has been associated with populism.

8. Nathan Hatch, *The Democratization of American Christianity* (New Haven: Yale University Press, 1989), 9.

9. Robert Lynd and Helen Lynd, *Middletown in Transition* (New York: Harcourt Brace Jovanovich Publishers, 1937), 295.

10. John Seel, "Creating a Parallel Universe: Telling Stories That Matter," *Wedgwood Circle*, February 2009.

11. James Davison Hunter, *Evangelicalism: The Coming Generation* (Chicago: University of Chicago Press, 1987), 151.

12. James Davison Hunter and Carl Bowman, "The Vanishing Center of American Democracy" (Charlottesville, VA: Advanced Studies in Cultural Foundation, 2016), 61, iasculture.org/research/publications /vanishing-center.

13. Deborah Jian Lee, *Rescuing Jesus: How People of Color, Women & Queer Christians Are Reclaiming Evangelicalism* (Philadelphia: Beacon, 2015).

14. Sarah Bessey, *Out of Sorts: Making Peace with an Evolving Faith* (New York: Howard Books, 2015); Evans, *Searching for Sunday*; Jen Hatmaker, *Interrupted: When Jesus Wrecks Your Comfortable Christianity* (Carol Stream, IL: NavPress, 2014); Nadia Bolz-Weber, *Accidental Saints: Finding God in All the Wrong People* (New York: Convergent, 2016).

CHAPTER 26: PAN-PAN

1. Dava Sobel, *Galileo's Daughter: A Historical Memoir of Science, Faith, and Love* (New York: Penguin, 2000).

2. Brian G. Murphy, "A Prayer for Wanderers," Queer Theology, accessed April 20, 2017, queertheology.com/prayer-wanderers/. Used with permission.

ABOUT THE AUTHOR

Photo Credit: David Hartcorn
Hartcorn Studios, Annapolis, Maryland
hartcornstudios.com

David John Seel, Jr., is a cultural-renewal entrepreneur and social-impact consultant. He works with people and projects that promote human flourishing and the common good. His expertise is in the dynamics of cultural change. He was the former director of cultural engagement at the John Templeton Foundation and is the founder of John Seel Consulting LLC. He has a PhD in American Studies from the University of Maryland (College Park), an MDiv from Covenant Theological Seminary, and a BA from Austin College.

John's interest in culture and cultural change came from his being the son of Presbyterian medical missionaries in South Korea. He lived overseas for seventeen years. He is a "third-culture-kid."

John has had a successful career in nonprofit and educational management. He worked for many years with evangelical author Os Guinness on The Williamsburg Charter as well as founding, with Guinness, The Trinity Forum. Later he served as administrative director for the Institute for Advanced Studies in Culture and research assistant professor at the University of Virginia, where he worked closely with sociologist James Davison Hunter. He also served as the founding headmaster of The Cambridge School of Dallas. More recently he has worked in entertainment and technology working with Walden Media, Scarlett City Studio, and nCore Media. He is active in Evangelicals for Social Action at Eastern University and is a senior advisor to the New Canaan Society and the Wedgwood Circle.

Though John attended a Presbyterian seminary, he has spent most of his adult life as an Anglican. The major spiritual influences in his life are C.S. Lewis, Francis Schaeffer, and Dallas Willard.

He is the father of three millennial children, Annie, David, and Alex, and the grandfather to four grandchildren. He is married to Kathryn and lives on a 450-acre historic farm in Philadelphia with their "four-legged child," an English-cream golden retriever named Malibu. He is active in Cresheim Valley Church (PCA). He enjoys writing, sailing, and sculling. He blogs three times per week on issues pertaining to millennials at www.ncconversations.com.